TRANSACTION TO ACTION –

THE CHIEF DATA OFFICER

Why some data leaders make the leap.....
and others don't

Anurakt Dixit

DISCLAIMER

The information presented in this book solely and fully represents the views of the author as of the date of publication. Any omission, or potential misrepresentation of, any peoples or companies, is entirely unintentional. As a result of changing information, conditions or contexts, this author reserves the right to alter content at his sole discretion impunity.

The book is for informational and advertising purposes only and while every attempt has been made to verify the information contained herein, the author assumes no responsibility for errors, inaccuracies, and omissions. Each person has unique needs and this book cannot take these individual differences into account. For ease of use, all links in this book are redirected through the link to facilitate any future changes and minimize dead links.

TABLE OF CONTENTS

DISCLAIMER i

INTRODUCTION 1

DIGITAL TRANSFORMATION 3

GETTING TO KNOW THE CDO 5

Who is a CDO? 5

Role Definition 6

Emerging From the Shadows 6

Transformational Change 7

The Responsibilities of the CDO 7

Driving business value 17

CDOs and the regulatory environment 22

Team dynamics 24

NEW HERO OF BIG DATA AND ANALYTICS 26

The emerging role of the Chief Data Officer 26

Areas In Which CDOs Can Turn Data Into Revenue 27

Connecting Strategic And Technical Objectives 30

Mind the gaps 33

VALUES OF A CHIEF DATA OFFICER 34

Top Motivations For Hiring A CDO 35

Solving Key Business Challenges 35

Breaking Down Data Barriers 36

DATA-DRIVEN TRANSFORMATION 37

You Need a Chief Data Officer. Here's why. 37

Ways a Chief Data Officer Drives Business Value 39

Creating a Data-Driven Organization Depends on a Data-Driven Culture 41

The Heartbeat Of A Data-Driven Culture 45

CREATING A DATA CULTURE 55

   Data Culture: The Missing Link in Your Data Strategy? 56

   Encourage, Engage and Educate 57

   Getting a Jump on Business: Where Data Cultures Are Already Succeeding 59

   Steps to Better Manage Data as an Asset 60

DECIDING TO HIRE A CDO 66

   Know Why You Want One 66

   Look for the Right Skill Set 67

THE CHALLENGES OF THE CDO 74

   Technical Challenges 74

   Business Challenges 78

   Political Challenges 81

   The art of the possible 82

   The art of persuasion 83

REPORTING LINES FOR THE CDO ROLE 85

   The CDO and the CIO 86

   Enter the Chief Risk Officer 89

   Data Stewards 91

LESSONS LEARNED FROM EARLY ADOPTERS 93

   Drive a C-suite mandate to take actions underpinned by data . 94

   Accelerating An Enterprise-Wide Data Strategy 96

   Reward Innovation That Drives Corporate Performance 98

   The Availability Gap 99

   Moving forward with the role of CDO 101

REFERENCES 103

INTRODUCTION

As the tide of "big data" continues to rise, organizations find themselves either comfortably riding the wave or up to their necks in new technologies and trying not to drown. As technology has come to play an increasingly vital role over the last several decades, the Chief Technology Officer (CTO) and Chief Information Officer (CIO) have become familiar roles. Now, the newer but rapidly spreading Chief Data Officer (CDO) position is becoming more familiar. And when provided the right structure and support, a CDO can be an excellent captain for navigating these new waters.

Many companies understand that data, when used correctly, can yield tremendous value—or even change entire industries. Just look at what Amazon or Netflix has done with recommendations, to take a "new school" web example, or what Walmart has done with supply chain optimization, to take an "old school" retail example. What company wouldn't want to achieve such results through data?

If those examples constitute the "carrot" of business insights, efficiency, and even brand new products, then there is also a data "stick." Industries such as finance and healthcare, which regularly deal with sensitive personal information, have become more heavily regulated regarding how they must handle and protect their data. Even without regulation, the ongoing plague of hacks has made the prospect of a large data breach a very scary possibility for anyone handling credit card transactions or other sensitive data.

Whether tempted by the carrot of new products and efficiencies or threatened by the stick of privacy and security concerns, many companies have elected to address these issues by appointing a CDO.

The role of CDO has been evolving rapidly over the last several years, and the consensus is beginning to emerge about how it can add the most value. You can still find a wide variety of implementations of the role of CDO: everything about the job, from reporting structure to primary responsibilities to required skill sets, can vary with the industry, company, and even the individual performing it. But there are some very distinct patterns and best practices, and some common threads that can yield guidance for those considering a CDO of their own. And for those organizations willing to put forth the effort and resources to lay the proper groundwork, there is a great deal of business value to be gained.

This book presents a picture of the current landscape, as well as how the Chief Data Officer helps an organization transition into a data-driven culture, some guidelines and best practices for those considering adding a CDO to their organization. I spoke with a dozen professionals who have performed the role in various settings including health-care, telecom, finance, marketing, insurance, and government at the municipal, state, and national levels. Their collected wisdom shows how the right data leadership can make companies more customers focused, competitive, and influential.

DIGITAL TRANSFORMATION

D ata is central to how we all live. As increasingly sophisticated technology and changing customer expectations usher in a wave of digital transformation, businesses will be turning to their data to power these initiatives. The overwhelming volume and variety of that data, however, can introduce more obstacles than it solves. Especially when it comes time to leverage it for business decisions or analyses. As organizations today grapple with this issue, they've come to realize one crucial lesson: data is only data until you make it actionable.

Making data actionable means that it needs to be accessible, accurate, and standardized. Therefore, it needs to be governed and managed appropriately over its life cycle. At many organizations today, the chief data officer (CDO) is responsible for ensuring that this process runs smoothly. Their core responsibility is to define a data management strategy and translate it into tactical, implementable steps for the business. By ensuring that data is high-quality and accessible, the CDO empowers business users with the information they need to make strategic decisions.

As it turns out, business users crave access to data—lots of data. Studies have found that nearly all of the CDOs agree that business stakeholders are demanding more access to data than ever before. Despite the tremendous demand for information, half of the CDOs I spoke to believe that while their data is a valuable business asset, they're not exploiting it to its full potential. That's why CDOs are focused on unlocking the power of their data through better data quality and data management. Doing so will enable sustainable programs that empower business users and drive digital transformation forward.

GETTING TO KNOW THE CDO

F ew would argue that information technology and data have become ingrained in nearly every aspect of today's business. Along the way - in no small part due to mobile phone contracts - they now have a major presence in our lives as consumers.

Indeed, for some organizations, today data has become such an explosive part of the business that they have created a Chief Data Officer (CDO) position to reside next to the Chief Information Officer and the Chief Technology Officer. This evolution acknowledges that data in the business setting is separate from the systems running it. Beyond that, it recognizes that data has a value that, if fully exploited, can help drive profitable business.

Who is a CDO?

A chief data officer (CDO) is a corporate officer responsible for enterprise-wide governance and utilization of information as an asset, via data processing, analysis, data mining, information trading and other means. CDOs report mainly to the chief executive officer

(CEO). Depending on the area of expertise this can vary. CDO is a member of the executive management team and manager of enterprise-wide data processing & data mining.

Role Definition

The Chief Data Officer title shares its abbreviation with the Chief Digital Officer, but the two are not the same job. The Chief Data Officer has a significant measure of business responsibility for determining what kinds of information the enterprise will choose to capture, retain and exploit and for what purposes.[1] However, the similar-sounding Chief Digital Officer or Chief Digital Information Officer often does not bear that business responsibility, but rather is responsible for the information systems through which data is stored and processed.

Emerging From the Shadows

For most of its history, data has been a shielded, hidden part of most businesses, too often lacking recognition as a value-add or business differentiator. Hard as it might be to believe today, for years it was typically the Head of Data Processing or the Data Processing Manager, who held responsibility for ensuring best data management practices across an enterprise. In practice, those roles, often very narrow regarding responsibility, could only be held by folks with very technical IT backgrounds and experience.

Then, sometime in the mid-80s/early 90s, the CIO role was created, in effect elevating a 'computing person' to the Board level for the first time. Still, data ownership fell into a gray area of overlap between a company's IT and operations departments - IT typically responsible for integration and data functions, operations typically responsible for ensuring that integrations ran smoothly.

Finally, a few leading firms have introduced a new role that bridges the gap between IT and operations and takes overall responsibility for data management: the Chief Data Officer.

Banking giant Wells Fargo, for example, just announced its first-ever CDO to manage the bank's enterprise data and analytics sector.

The rise of the CDO is a testament to the growing importance that firms are placing on the value of data and data management across the enterprise. More than that, the CDO is giving data a permanent seat at the executive table.

Transformational Change

The rise of the Chief Data Officer is a transformational change that elevates the importance of data to the top of the organization. Giving the role of data management a seat at the C-suite table allows organizations to be transparent when it comes to the real cost components of data and the value that data can play in various parts of the organization. It's a view that has long been missing from the corporate agenda.

The Responsibilities of the CDO

A Gartner study of large global enterprises indicated that the number of CDOs doubled between 2014 and 2015. It suggests that by 2020, 25% of them will have appointed a chief data officer. Even as the number of CDOs grows, we find that the scope and expectations of the CDO role continue to evolve. Firms are continuing to refine how the role should play out, how to build consensus on the use of data at the business-unit and enterprise levels, and what approach makes the most sense for them.

We analyzed CDO trends and conducted in-depth discussions with executives in key financial institutions to gain insight into how the role of the CDO is evolving in today's environment.

While CDO responsibilities vary by organization, they typically cover:

Data architecture and technology

Data architecture is a collection of blueprints designed to standardize how data is sourced, integrated, and consumed across the enterprise and aligned with the business strategy. Technology refers to the infrastructure needed to build those blueprints: for example, data warehouses, Big Data platforms, and data integration tools.

Data analytics

This is a function that helps companies gain insight and perspective from their data. It includes real-time business intelligence, analytics, and reporting services. In mature organizations, this function has evolved into a shared services capability that provides robust data management and analytics capabilities in a cost-effective way. This reduces operational cost, fosters the reuse of data across the enterprise, and improves turnaround time.

Most financial firms view the CDO role as one that should function at the enterprise level to foster tone-from-the-top and uniformity across the organization. But starting at the enterprise level can be daunting and costly, both regarding budget and time. As a result, some organizations have embarked on smaller-scale efforts by creating the CDO role at the business-unit or functional level (such as Risk or Finance). While these efforts lack the benefits that many firms value in a centralized model, they can be implemented more quickly and serve as a stepping stone for the enterprise-wide rollout. And they can allow executives to focus on areas where intervention is needed most urgently.

Breadth

The first overarching theme is that the CDO is a very broad role. Those who fill it must focus on a wide variety of tasks, and be able to consider everyday tactical details as well as the bigger strategic picture. The job is about mapping the particulars of a company's data needs to its overall business purpose to create and drive value and about working successfully with all divisions across the organization to ensure that everyone is pulling in the same direction.

"You have to do, enable, and govern," said Charles Thomas, CDO of Wells Fargo. "You do a few big broad things; you enable the technology, tools, skillsets that you provide to the enterprise; and you govern far more."

❖ At Wells Fargo, Thomas and his team are responsible for overseeing the entire data lifecycle, from obtaining data to acting on it. This lifecycle is often referred to as the "data value chain." It's sometimes described with its stages broken down in differing ways, but at its core, it includes: Discovering a set of relevant data, acquiring access to that data (both from a rights perspective and a technical perspective).

❖ Ingesting data into the data warehouse, which may require wrangling diverse file formats.

❖ Processing the data to transform it as necessary and ensure that the proper metadata is available.

❖ Persisting the data across an appropriate storage platform so that it can be shared and reused.

❖ Integrating the data with other data sources to unlock insights from the relationships between disparate data sets.

❖ Analyzing the data to understand the patterns and relationships in it, and figuring out how to employ those insights in an operational way.

❖ Exposing the insights to others in the organization and encouraging the relevant decision-makers to execute on the intelligence.

Not every CDO role is so all-encompassing; as we'll see in a moment, some CDOs play a coordinating role that leaves responsibility for early parts of the data value chain with other areas of the business. What's important to understand is toward the end of the data value chain: if the role stops short of yielding operational execution, then its potential impact is not fully realized.

Balance

The second overarching theme is that the CDO must find and maintain balance: between ideal strategies and practical implementations, between short- and long-term budget concerns, and among competing for divisional priorities. To achieve this balance often requires great diplomacy and the ability to collaborate with others while educating them on evolving tools, techniques, and landscapes.

Micheline Casey, former CDO of the Federal Reserve Board, said of her role there: "What I am setting up my team to do—and thus educating my senior advisory committee on—is about this balance between strategic needs of the organization with moving things forward in agile ways so we begin to add value early, and to help them understand what agile means."

Casey's role was created by the Federal Reserve's Strategic Framework 2012–2015, which contains a section on data governance. In addition to fulfilling the strategic objectives laid out in that document, Casey looked for ways to enhance the data their economists have access to. Most of the data the Federal Reserve System tracks is historical, so Casey pursued ways to balance that with external data that could be more real-time or even predictive. She also worked to set up a Data Lab that could support the process of identifying new data sets, tools, and methods to enable cutting-edge approaches that would balance the institution's more traditional methods.

Centralization

Enterprise-scale companies may consist of dozens or even hundreds of smaller companies or divisions. And each of these produces data. The CDO is in charge of making the data available across these different silos and bringing it into one central place—with some set of standardized formats—so that it can be analyzed and put to maximum use.

While not every organization does it this way yet, there's a strong argument for centralizing data: value comes from going outside of traditional silos and combining multiple data sources to get to better insights—for example, combining CRM data with website data to understand which customers make certain decisions and have better experiences. Having a centralized executive, the CDO, who is free to focus on extracting value from data, allows the organization to unlock value by making investments that none of the silo owners would make individually because the return on investment exists only for the enterprise as a whole.

Azarias Reda is former CDO of the Republican National Committee (RNC), which does fundraising and marketing as well as voter profiling to help with party elections in many different districts, states, and constituencies. They also run a website, GOP.com, which appeals to would-be voters with everything from leadership surveys and discussion of the Keystone Pipeline to brightly colored socks bearing the signature of former President George H.W. Bush. The site is a place to both gather and distributes data-driven research.

"A lot of our work, actually, has to do with collecting this data for all the states and going through a process to make it uniform and nationally accessible," said Reda. "One of the first areas that emerged for us was creating a unified center for collecting our data from multiple sources within the organization itself so that we could build a better picture of who the voter is."

Whether you're talking about voters, patients, or customers, the goal now is often to establish a "360° view" of who each person is. The argument is that aggregation is not only good for the business, enabling the more holistic use of data, but it is also good for the customer.

Anyone who has used a customer loyalty card and come to expect personalized coupons or the occasional free cup of coffee made just the way they like it has experienced this 360° customer view—and the data required to achieve it—in action.

"No matter who you deal with, whether it is a retailer, or whether it is a financial institution, we have all become trained (and rightly so) to expect to be treated as a person and not a series of products," said

Floyd Yager, CDO of Allstate. In addition to overseeing core data quality and management issues for the Allstate's auto and homeowners business (a line of business that constitutes about 85% of their revenue), his role involves thinking ahead about what the company should be doing with data over a three-year horizon. And achieving the holistic customer view is at the top of his list.

The problem is that, since this kind of approach is still relatively new, the process of aggregating that data requires a lot of work. Most traditional companies are optimized to look at each product, service, or group with its attendant data in its silo.

"We have very good data, but it is organized to help us run our business the way we have run our business for 80-some years," said Yager. "I need to take all of the data that was very transactionally efficient to help process an auto insurance policy, and join it to all of my homeowner's data, all of my life insurance data, all of my commercial insurance data, and everything else I have. So that when Joe Smith calls me, I can look at Joe Smith as that unit, rather than Joe Smith's auto policy."

Of course, it takes a lot of time, money, and people power to overhaul legacy systems and to integrate data from so many different internal sources. And integration or aggregation are much better terms than centralization when talking about the data, as very often the pre-existing data-generating systems are left intact. But the theme at work here in the role of the CDO is bigger than just aggregating data: it is also about centralizing the strategic role of data in the organization.

Prioritization

If the CDO is going to be the central point of support for business goals, then they must also take the lead in determining company priorities for data-driven projects. This may be partly a matter of resource allocation, but it is also about taking a broad view of upcoming projects and priorities in disparate parts of the organization.

"If you do it the right way and you take an enterprise view, how you build the data and how you do the project can make it easier for the next project to be done," said Yager, "even if it is in a different area of responsibility. Prioritization becomes integration, and not just completing that one task, but how you complete it to make the enterprise work more smoothly."

At the University of South Carolina, CDO Mike Kelly is working to implement a five-part framework set forth by members of their data administration advisory committee. The framework is broad and ambitious, especially in an academic setting without the deep pockets of a Fortune 500 company. So implementing pieces of it in the right order is vital for success.

"We live in a resource-constrained time, and in a time when there is no shortage of good ideas, and imperatives, and compliance requirements," says Kelly. "So, sometimes we have to look and say, What's the most important thing—or couple things—that we can and will invest our time and effort in, and move that ball forward?"

Sometimes prioritization is simply a matter of listening to the project leads across departments and creating a central project list from which to distill a plan of attack. But it can also be a more nuanced problem than that: often, it is as political as it is strategic for the business. Choosing the right project with which to demonstrate the utility and efficacy of certain approaches and tools can help get people on board for the next project, and set the whole organization up for future success; or not.

"One of the things that were very clear in the literature [on data governance]," says Kelly, "is you need a quick win to get and keep executive buy-in." In the best case, the executive team will already be sold on the importance of data and the insights and products it can drive, but being able to demonstrate value right away can make a difference to maintaining that top-down support.

Equally important is achieving the buy-in of colleagues across various departments. At Zynga, CDO Amy Gershkoff helps her team use clear communication and ask probing questions to keep their sights set on the right priorities without getting pulled down rabbit holes.

When working with various business units, "I always tell my analysts and data scientists not to run the query they were asked to run," says Gershkoff, "but rather to turn around and ask their business partner what business question they are trying to answer. And that has led to some really exciting and impactful results."

This focus on prioritizing data projects is a defining feature of the CDO role, whether it happens directly or more diffusely by exerting influence and evangelizing a data-driven mindset.

Evangelization

The most effective CDO team is not a new department that is simply appended onto the old way of doing things, like a third arm that adds incremental capability. It is more like developing a nerve system: it works with all the other parts of the organism, collecting information and passing signals back and forth in a way that allows for better collective action and decision-making. A nervous system is not made of muscle; its job is to inform and influence, not to act all by itself.

The CDO's team is typically quite small compared to the rest of the enterprise, so convincing others in the organization that this kind of work is worth investing in—convincing them to be the muscle that does the heavy lifting—is critical to success. The CDO must be an advocate for data-driven approaches generally, and individual projects specifically, and must achieve buy-in from colleagues on many levels of the organizational hierarchy. This requires a certain amount of visibility.

Rob Alderfer is former CDO of the Wireless Telecommunications Bureau at the FCC (Federal Communications Commission). "The role of CDO is enhanced by close alignment with the goals of the agency or the organization. So rather than being seen as the data geek who is off doing his own thing, if you are seen as using data as an integral piece of a larger common goal, that is what gets people's attention," said Alderfer.

There are several ways to organize data scientists within a company: they may be their centralized team reporting to the CDO; they may work together collaboratively from positions embedded in other business units, or they may be fully distributed among the various departments with deep domain expertise. Many organizations who are hiring data scientists for the first time begin with a more centralized model and then slowly integrate them into other business units. During this early phase, visibility may be a challenge, so the CDO's role as an evangelist and ambassador is particularly critical at the beginning.

Of course, to be an effective ambassador, you also have to be able to speak the same language as the person you are trying to win over to your cause. The ideal CDO is fluent in both business and technical matters—but more importantly, can translate between the two.

Scott Kaylie, former CDO of QuestPoint, believes the language bar- river is more than metaphorical. "Even if a DBA [database administrator] and marketing professionals are using the same words, they could have very different meanings," said Kaylie. For example, he said, when talking about a group of website or application users, a word as simple as all can have two different meanings. To a marketing professional, it may mean "every single user that exists," but to a DBA, it may mean "every user except these excluded ones, who are in the middle of testing."

For a CDO, who must work with stakeholders from all parts of the company, successful evangelization comes from "being able to speak both of those languages, to understand the business concepts that will drive the profitability of the business, and being able to talk intelligently with the technology teams," said Kaylie.

Facilitation

Of course, even as you're winning everyone over to the importance of working with data in new ways, you also have to remove existing barriers and free up the resources to make it feasible. The ideal CDO is one who makes better, more efficient action possible for the rest of the organization.

"Part of the job was to represent the resource needs for data practices within the priorities of the agency," said former FCC Wireless Telecommunications Bureau CDO Rob Alderfer. "A lot of the stuff I am talking about, though, is not necessarily money: it is just people's time."

Alderfer's work focused on using data to both encourage public participation in the policy process and improve policy outcomes. From regularly publishing data via an API to releasing the data from an internal report in an accompanying spreadsheet file, he said, institutionalizing open data practices within the agency adds extra work for everyone involved, not just those on the CDO's team. So part of his job was to make that as easy and obvious as possible. But, he added, "The fact that the FCC had a chief data officer represents a commitment of resources in and of itself."

Joy Bonaguro, CDO of San Francisco City and County, also discussed the commitment required from all involved. She regularly convenes analysts and stakeholders from the whole municipality to identify and discuss their challenges in implementing open data and with working internally with sensitive constituent data. San Francisco maintains a website, DataSF, that acts as a clearinghouse for public data, including data about transportation, public safety, health and social services, housing, energy, and many other widely varying topics. "Because it's a new role and there were all these existing things going on, my strategy with resourcing has been to emphasize the coordination instead of trying to have a bunch of stuff to me," she said.

In addition to coordinating disparate departments, facilitating action is about providing new tools and lowering the bar to the kind of tasks you're asking others to do. "The city has a lot of great work that's happening. Learning about that made me realize that I need to enable this work to continue to happen," said Bonaguro. "I think I initially came in thinking, 'Maybe we need to provide analytical services to departments.' What I found is that it's better in a lot of ways to have those within the departments." Her team focuses on providing support to the city's divisions by developing toolkits and offering training.

Another method of facilitation, especially within government, is contributing to policy. "The FCC budget is about $450 million a year, but it regulates an industry that is in the hundreds of billions regarding economic impact," said Alderfer. "So if you can have an impression on the broader economic impact from a policy perspective, then that's really where it probably makes sense to focus most of your time. I spent a lot of my time at the FCC figure out how to improve the data that was used in policy decisions."

Driving business value

All these complexities, along with a clear business need for the data function to be managed, leads to a conundrum for the C-suite: Who should be taking care of the data function?

Increasingly, organizations are answering that question by creating the Chief Data Officer role. And the resulting CDOs are delivering on an executive mandate to manage scarce resources efficiently and address complex business challenges in their quest to leverage enterprise data. Through governance of data policy, their organizations can gain important stakeholders, marshal resources and focus the organization to do things it might not otherwise be able to do with its data.

While specific priorities vary based on an organization's business goals, today's CDOs serve common priorities across multiple organizations, such as cost reductions, compliance and revenue enhancement (see Figure 1). And there is broad agreement on one overarching priority: leveraging enterprise data to drive business value.

Mandates of the office of the CDO

What it means to drive business value from data varies by organization, industry and geographic span. For example, for companies that provide information services, data is directly related to revenue. For governmental organizations, sharing, collaboration, re-use and openness of data are key. In an information services scenario, data is managed as a product, and a CDO might have responsibility for identifying new sources of data and determining how to package existing data, from internal or external sources, to create commercial offerings.

In most organizations, however, the linkage between data and revenue or impact isn't quite so direct. While most organizations don't sell data, they do sell or provide goods or services that rely on timely, accurate information. The CDO's key objectives may range from defining the best ways to leverage existing, internal data to finding and exploiting new data sources from existing or new business partners or big data sources, such as machine data or social media.

Research revealed several companies that have appointed the CDO as the board-mandated champion to listen to the front line, data stewards and customers to resolve conflicts and remove any transformation success barriers. They understand that a data-centric or analytics-driven transformation isn't a one-step trip; on the contrary, it is an ongoing journey with a series of destinations — each a staging post for the next.

Ursula Cottone, Chief Data Officer at KeyBank, has found that across the organization, there is a need for a new way of thinking about data as an asset unto itself, as distinguished from the systems where it resides. People often think of data as technology, she says, but getting them to think of data in business terms can be a challenge.

From a corporate culture perspective, the CDO can be a change agent. To embrace the many possibilities a CDO can support, organizations need to ask themselves new questions about data and how it could benefit them.

"I am convinced that data and information will change the way Philips will evolve in the coming decade," explains Bart Luijten, Senior Vice President and Global Head of Enterprise Information Management at Royal Dutch Philips. "The way in which we will be able to use and leverage that data, and the way I can combine it with other data, defines the shape and size of the business opportunities that come along... Philips intends to use data actually to improve people's lives," he adds.

Looking for superheroes

The CDO is a business executive, not a technician, programmer or data scientist. While the global shortage of data scientists has been intensely covered in the media, the CDO is soon to become the next "hot job," and the skills are vastly different. Data scientists typically have backgrounds as mathematicians, statisticians, and behavioral psychologists.

A CDO, on the other hand, not only understands the industry and market within which the organization is competing but also has technical knowledge of data, its structures, and its potential as an asset.

CDOs need a "T-shaped" skills set

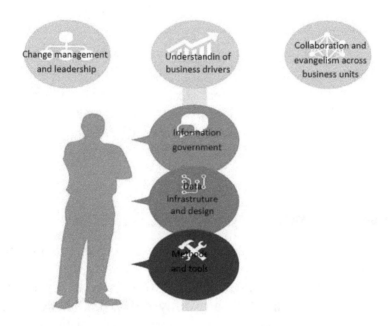

Figure: CDOs need to combine business, technology, and people skills to drive change management, evangelism and strong collaboration across the organization.

A successful CDO possesses a balance of technical skills, business knowledge, and people skills and works effectively with the CIO — but not as a replacement for the CIO — to manage data and make it useable.

Based on my experiences and interviews, I determined that the most successful CDOs are tasked with providing the business knowledge needed to deliver the vision, strategy, and oversight, as well as budget management responsibilities, for all the organization's initiatives related to data, including new business opportunities. But that's not all. CDOs are equally tasked with leading, managing and nurturing teams of data scientists, data aggregators and others with the business and technical skills to identify the opportunities data can create.

"One thing I've found is that it takes not only a good understanding of the business, the business needs and the market drivers," explains Ashok Srivastava, Chief Data Scientist for Verizon, "but also a good understanding of the data, machine learning, and other advanced technologies. Then, bringing all these things together is a key aspect of having a good data science team."

CDOs interviewed echoed Srivastava's experience, noting they must have enough business savvy to drive the conversation on the strategic value of data. But also have sufficient technical skills to oversee data workflows, data sources, data vendor capabilities, data definitions, data access and other data-related issues, as well as establish and enforce data policies and standards.

As collaborators and facilitators of data usage, CDOs also need sharp skills in negotiation and leadership to maintain a healthy collaboration with other parts of the data function, including product development, corporate strategy and analysis, research and development, and shared service centers like analytics centers of competence. As they drive innovation and revenue, successful CDOs have managed to change the perception of their role from sole organizational data owner to that of steward of enterprise information and information models.

Of course, there will always be business leaders who are reluctant to relinquish control of their information silos to a central data officer. While a CDO typically seeks to rationalize data across the organization — at least to understand what it is, where it is and how it can be leveraged to drive the business — those who manage their data silos may not initially see the advantage of increased openness, collaboration and access to their data from individuals and systems outside their sphere of control.

In the end, mandated CDOs — those with support from the CEO — need to build and maintain alliances with other C-level officers and groups of the organization to be effective. For that reason, strong leadership, organizational change management, and a collaborative style are all important CDO characteristics.

Research reveals that the typical CDO has a graduate degree and more than ten years' business experience combined with extensive — and often overlapping — data experience in areas such as architecture and governance. According to Gartner, there are CDOs in more than a dozen countries today, though 65 percent are in the United States and 20 percent in the United Kingdom.

CDOs by geography

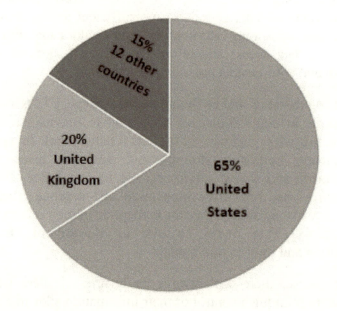

Figure: CDOs are largely concentrated in the United States today, but that is expected to change over the next few years.

CDOs and the regulatory environment

While many organizations are prepared to address audit, compliance and regulatory requirements through their boards and oversight committees, Chief Data Officers look at the requirements differently.

CDOs see regulatory and compliance requirements as a mandate to implement best practices in managing a business and its data, turning an otherwise onerous task into one that drives business value. They take a broad view, driving data discipline to deliver capital and risk management and privacy benefits, as well as business performance measures.

Some smart CDOs are using funding of compliance and regulatory projects as a "Trojan horse" to launch efforts to consolidate data, conform tools, align processes and organizations, and establish a data policy.

In the first organizational model, CDOs report directly to the Chief Executive Officer, which elevates data ownership to the CEO's agenda and creates a stronger mandate for a data-driven transformation. This alignment drives an organization toward business enablement and innovation. However, we also find that it can create a power conflict between the CIO and the CDO unless roles are defined, and collaboration is emphasized. We see this model used extensively within financial service organizations.

In the second model, the CDO is a direct report to the CIO, thereby removing the political conflict. Appropriate in organizations where there is strong IT leadership, this structure makes it easier to coordinate data management with the enterprise architecture and integrate it into the infrastructure. The drawback is that data can quickly be de-emphasized as the organization continues to focus on its hardware and software needs. We find this model most frequently in the retail industry and other customer-centric organizations.

Debra Logan of Gartner advocates that CIOs should view the CDO as a peer and partner who can manage data and who has the knowledge, background, and skills to do so, which allows CIOs to focus on "the more-than-full-time job" that they already have managed the organization's technology and infrastructure.

In the third organizational model, the CDO is a direct report to some other C-level executive. While diminishing the link to the

CEO, this model emphasizes a business-driven data agenda that is separate from the architecture and infrastructure mandate of IT. It supports a more collaborative approach to driving business outcomes from data in organizations where there may be a disparity in power between business and IT. I observed this model being used across a wide variety of industries.

Regardless of reporting structure, positive and collaborative relationships with the both the CEO and CIO are critical for the CDO. Foremost, the CEO needs to establish the value of data to the organization and the value of the CDO in leading the organization to optimize the benefits of all available data.

Team dynamics

CDOs most often require a team with business and technology skills that reflect those of the CDO. The strongest performers from the CIO's or CTO's team are not necessarily strong candidates for new positions created under the CDO. Instead, the best candidate may be the "renaissance person" who truly understands the business, but also has familiarity with technology and superb communication skills. That combination is not easy to find.

As a result, it may be hard for CDOs to build teams with the right combination of capabilities. CDO Mario Faria sums it up this way: What's needed is individuals who possess:

❖ Business skills — for understanding business in general and the specific corporate priorities in particular.

❖ Communication skills — for effective collaboration across the organization.

❖ Process skills — for effecting change and implementing new processes.

❖ Technology understanding — for defining possibilities but not for programming.

Prior publications reveal that it is doable to find technical understanding or business skills separately or even to grow those skills quickly within the organization.16 The unique T-shaped skills set of understanding the business data, understanding the tools and techniques to deploy, and articulating critical messages about data on a senior management level remains a rare find.

Cultivating duo teams of skilled business and technical people, complemented with an external coaching model, seems to be a best practice for creating successful teams. As Mark Ramsey, CDO at Samsung Telecommunications America points out; data science is a hot field that is attracting interest. There are not a lot of individuals with the right skill combinations available, and there is competition for those people. Some candidates bring skills from academics or government or analytics but lack business experience. Ramsey, for instance, looks for business skills plus some of those other skills, in areas like data science, analytics and even platforms like Hadoop. The bottom line is that the team needs to excel at the application of data to solve business problems and open new business opportunities.

NEW HERO OF BIG DATA AND ANALYTICS

The Chief Data Officer

T he Chief Data Officer is a business leader who creates and executes data and analytics strategies to drive business value. The role is responsible for defining, developing and implementing the strategy and methods by which the organization acquires, manages, analyzes and governs data. It also carries the strategic responsibility to drive the identification of new business opportunities through more effective and creative use of data.

The emerging role of the Chief Data Officer

Over the last decade, most organizations have become increasingly dependent on data — for recording their business transactions, managing their production lines and defining their growth strategies. A deluge of data has created the need for new skill sets, but it isn't clear just which specialists can save the day and enable organizations to act in time to tap the data opportunity. Although it is data that creates both the problem and the new opportunity for growth and innovation, organizations tend to turn to technology as the solution.

What's missing is clarity of vision around the data itself — who owns it, what it means, how it should be managed and how it can be monetized — or, in governmental practice, how it can lead to better service and data reuse. Most data problems result from an initial failure to plan, followed by a failure to address the proliferation of data. And unclear data ownership, lack of a common business language, siloed thinking and a focus on short-term projects and exciting "silver bullet" technologies obscure the solutions. Along with these artifacts related to an absence of executive information governance, lack of innovative thinking is also holding organizations back, keeping them from recognizing market opportunities that simply didn't exist before the introduction of new sources of data. Now organizations are faced with scoping and managing large-scale transformations to correct decades of unbridled, unmanaged data expansion without a corresponding expansion of vision.

Areas In Which CDOs Can Turn Data Into Revenue

As the digitization of business and consumerism changes the volume, velocity, and variety of data, business needs are changing as well. Moving beyond an era in which data was used to "sense and respond" to business activities, enterprises now want to use data to "predict and act," creating a more flexible and forward-looking organization. In this environment, business executives are making data-driven decisions, based on high-quality, high-volume, real-time data available at the points of impact.

This business evolution highlights several opportunities and issues that drive the requirement to create a C-level position to oversee an organization's data assets: data leverage, data monetization, data enrichment, data upkeep and data protection. Let's explore these topics:

Data leverage involves finding ways to use existing data assets to advance the cause of the organization. The objective may be to uplift operational efficiency or productivity, boost the brand image, improve top-line revenue, or innovate for competitive differentiation and analytic advantage. One of the first justification we heard for creating the role of a CDO was ensuring that an organization is designed to make data-driven decisions — hence, the need for an executive who drives the organization to focus on leveraging data and addressing some fundamental questions:

❖ How can we do more with the data we have?

❖ How can we augment that data, by supplementing and complementing it with data from partnerships or other external sources?

❖ How can we derive viable insights from that data?

❖ How can we take advantage of those insights in the existing business model?

❖ How can we leverage those insights across existing and new business partnerships?

❖ How can those insights open new opportunities and business models for our organization?

Seven out of twelve CDOs interviewed said they were able to create "low-hanging fruit" successes through data leverage by deriving meaningful information and viable insights from data that already existed within their organization. Sometimes they even created new business models whereby the data could be sold, leased or used to create additional enterprise offerings and revenue streams.

Hence, **data monetization** is an extension of data leverage that focuses on finding new avenues of earnings and revenue opportunities outside existing processes and functions — very often with direct impact on existing business models and organizational strategy.

For example, a bank may be looking to monetize its credit card data to open new revenue streams by selling insights to its ecosystem partners, within the customer-approved privacy framework. A telecommunications company might augment its location data with other customer demographics to offer more convenient mobile banking. And a mobile handset manufacturing company could try to collaborate or bypass the telecom service providers for new revenue through mobile channel advertising dollars. We observed successful CDOs focused on doing the right things, including integrating and collecting the right data, to leverage and monetize this strategic asset.

Often relying on the revenue or savings created through better data leverage and monetization, the next opportunity CDOs tackle is **data enrichment**, whereby existing datasets are augmented through the combination of fragmented internal data sources, the acquisition of external data from government feeds or social media sources and the integration of a business partner's data.

Data upkeep refers to managing the health of the data under governance. With the growing data explosion and data mashing over websites, companies, and consumers, there is a clear need for new and different methods that address data quality and governance as a positive differentiator for customers and citizens. The CDO is ultimately accountable for multiple aspects of data maintenance like data integrity, veracity, value, semantics and overall health.

Data protection is a special aspect of data upkeep. It is of paramount importance to any organization, given the high risks associated with failure to protect data as an asset. If the one who has the data is the king, then the king needs to protect his kingdom. Typically, this protection is exercised through collaboration with another executive role responsible for information security, a.k.a. The Chief Information Security Officer (CISO).

Addressing these requirements, the Chief Data Officer takes the lead in making the best data from within and beyond the organization available in a well-governed environment to help the organization steer a winning competitive course, strategic and attuned to the objectives of the enterprise.

A socially adjusted inventory

As the executive in charge of big data and analytics project, the CDO of a global retailer launched a major effort to combine unstructured external data with internal point-of-sale data to create a complete data picture.

With the desired business outcome of more accurately forecasted inventory needs, the CDO predicted answers could be found within social media chatter. By marrying the two data-sets — and focusing on data enrichment and data protection — the CDO used social sentiment analysis to answer key consumer questions relating to what kind of electronics devices people sought and whether those choices varied by store location.

The result was a data leverage approach applied to inventory on its way to the distribution center. This socially adjusted operation resulted in a forecast 24 percent closer to actual sales than previous models, uplift in actual sales and a decrease in later markdowns, all without ordering more items.

Connecting Strategic And Technical Objectives

Once the evolution of a new way of thinking is started, a different challenge emerges. Individuals across various departments are eager to seize new possibilities but have trouble articulating just what it is they need from data. For example, CDO Ursula Cottone has seen a big increase in demand for data of all types, whether from internal sources like unstructured documents or e-mail or external sources like social media.

As a result, the CDO team needs to move from inspiring new possibilities to provide more practical guidance for developing concrete plans and a roadmap for moving through various phases from the current state to the desired state where data is driving business growth. At this point, the CDO needs change agent and negotiation skills to gather requirements across multiple functional areas, assess needs and set priorities for the data roadmap.

The development and execution of an overall data strategy for the organization is a key responsibility of the CDO. That strategy might address issues like data ownership, data sources and data quality, as well as the scope and structure of the organization focused on data. After creating such a strategy, the CDO then prioritizes execution, first by creating the team that reports to the CDO.

Along with such a journey, many questions will emerge. Companies must be prepared to make the numerous changes — in both processes and corporate culture — that are required. In their quest to become more data-centric, many organizations initiate an enterprise-wide analytics transformation program, which is often led by the Chief Data Officer. In the program's infancy, CDO priorities include setting up new organizational structures, creating and running governance processes and committees, and overseeing certain in-flight initiatives.

One of-the-moment issue for CDOs involves consideration of a cloud environment. With the ability to increase efficiency and lower operating costs, the prospect of a cloud-based environment — whether used to house business process, software, platform components or the entire data infrastructure — not only opens up new opportunities for a broader range of organizations but is something that few organizations can afford to ignore.

Data challenges themselves vary by organization and so do the priorities of those responsible for solving them. In many organizations, often where years of data integration efforts have created a chaotic data environment, CDOs immediately focus on improving data quality.

A technical or business background can assist a CDO in addressing data quality effectively; however, a clear understanding of the business domain, as well as desire, passion, and imagination to take the organization to the next level, are even more important.

Over time, however, the CDO priorities typically become more strategic, as he or she increasingly collaborates with top business leaders to determine how timely, high-quality data can support top-level business goals, and then makes it happen. As this transition from tactical to strategic occurs, CDOs often create new and improve existing processes for information governance.

In some organizations — typically larger ones — the CDO is at the helm of a formal information governance structure, with advisory committees, an information governance council, and multiple stewards of data across different domains. Other organizations adopt the concept of information governance but have a less formal structure. In those cases, the CDO acts as an advisor for governance processes, but the processes are managed without the benefit of advisory committees, councils or stewards.

This research did not reveal a single best practice for the fit of a CDO within an organization. However, three prevalent models did emerge that link the CDO to the CEO, the CIO or another CxO. Each alignment approach offers different benefits and allows a company to act according to its priorities.

Even while interest in governance is growing in the era of big data, some organizations practice what I call "stealth data governance." Mario Faria, CDO for a cloud services organization, shared that in his organization, "...there is no formal data governance council. If I called a meeting of a group by that name, no executive would come." But he believes it is important to have complete transparency with executives. So he calls meetings by other names, gets executives into a room, and then discusses key issues and activities related to information governance.

Similarly, the Chief Data Officer for an international insurance and financial services organization says, "The word governance — people become deaf to it." What's important is the value that can be delivered by well-governed data, she explains.

Mind the gaps

Though the CDO is expected to exercise executive authority over data, the lens through which the role is viewed can significantly impact some considerations:

❖ Is the CDO aligned to the business or technology?

❖ Is the CDO an influencing role or an owner?

❖ Is the CDO a guiding or enforcing authority?

❖ Is the CDO a leader of compliance and regulatory activity?

Some of these questions may be answered differently based on time and circumstances. For example, a U.S. bank under intense regulatory scrutiny might answer the questions differently from a manufacturing organization seeking to increase operational efficiency.

VALUES OF A CHIEF DATA OFFICER

As organizations continue to rely on their data to drive business initiatives, the responsibilities placed on the CDO will increase as well. In fact, 63 percent of the CDOs we interviewed said that they feel an increased responsibility for data management compared to just one year ago.

In light of the growing focus on data-driven initiatives by the business, the attention devoted to data management is a necessary step toward making data more readily accessible. To that end, our study revealed that nearly half of CDOs (49%) say that over the last year they've felt increased pressure to provide data faster to business stakeholders.

You might be inclined to think that the increase in pressure on the CDO would give way to feelings of being under-appreciated and over-worked. To the contrary, I found that CDOs today feel that the value they can contribute to their business has increased over a year ago.

Additionally, when we asked chief information officers (CIOs) about the impact that CDOs have on their businesses, a majority of them (88%) said the role adds value to their data management strategy—an increase of 2 percent from two years ago. It's clear that businesses with CDOs in place understand the tangible value the role adds to their organization.

Top Motivations For Hiring A CDO

The volume and variety of data that organizations collect and manage today are growing at an accelerating rate, and this makes governing and managing that information increasingly complex. As the demands around data management have evolved over the years, CIOs are finding that they simply do not have the resources to keep up.

This is especially the case for organizations without a CDO role in place. My study revealed that more than two-thirds of CIOs (76%) who do not have a CDO in place at their organization say that their current role fails to cover the majority of responsibilities a CDO would have—an increase of 8 percent from two years ago.

What does that mean? Organizations without a CDO are not effectively harnessing the potential of their data because, among other factors, CIOs are simply spread too thin. In fact, many of the data innovation projects that a CDO would undertake are not getting done.

That said, I am encouraged to see that a majority of CIOs (82%) believe that there is a compelling business case to hire a CDO in most organizations today.

Solving Key Business Challenges

Over the next two years, CDOs predict that the top business challenges will be around improving data security, keeping pace with technology advances, and managing increased customer expectations.

Meeting these business challenges requires data that is high-quality and readily accessible. While 96 percent of CDOs say that their business stakeholders are demanding more access to data assets, only 10 percent of CDOs describe their ability to exploit available data to drive the business forward as excellent.

Breaking Down Data Barriers

Why are so many organizations unable to leverage the data they have? There are many reasons for this—-chief among them is the ability (or lack thereof) to access data. Furthermore, limited budgets to invest in data platforms and skilled staff coupled with the volume of information can make it nearly impossible for organizations to exploit their data, even with a CDO in place.

When comparing the responses from the CDO to those of the CIO, we noticed that the ability to access data varies widely. In fact, CIOs see the volume of data as a greater barrier to the business's ability to exploit data. Given that CIOs typically oversee the IT side of the organization, it makes sense that they have access to the data. However, as the CDO role sits between lines of business and IT, they have flagged a clear problem, which is that business users do not have access to that same information. Typically they must submit requests to the IT department and wait hours or even days for that data.

For CDOs to begin tackling their business challenges, they need to focus on resolving these barriers,- starting with improving access to data.

DATA-DRIVEN
TRANSFORMATION

You Need a Chief Data Officer. Here's why.

C DOs play a critical role in data-driven transformation. But only if they're set up to succeed.

Big data has moved from buzzword to being a part of everyday life within enterprise organizations. An IDG survey reports that 75% of enterprise organizations have deployed or plan to deploy big data projects. The challenge now is capturing strategic value from that data and delivering high-impact business outcomes.

That's where a Chief Data Officer (CDO) enters the picture. Gartner estimates that 90% of large global organizations will have a CDO by 2021. Given that estimate, it's important for CIOs and the rest of the C-suite to understand how a CDO can deliver maximum impact for data-driven transformation.

While the first generation of CDOs were brought on to oversee data governance and data management, their role is transitioning into one focused on how to best organize and use data as a strategic asset within organizations. But many CDOs still don't have the resources, budget, or authority to drive digital transformation on their own, so the CDO needs to help the CIO drive transformation via collaboration and evangelism.

"The CDO should not just be part of the org chart, but also have an active hand in launching new data initiatives," Patricia Skarulis, SVP & CIO of Memorial Sloan Kettering Cancer Center, said at the recent CIO Perspectives conference in New York.

What, When, How

A few months ago, I was involved in a conversation with the leadership team of a large organization. This conversation revolved around whether they needed to hire a CDO and, if they did, what that individual's role should be. It's always difficult creating a new role, especially one like the CDO whose oversight spans multiple departments. To create this role (and have the person succeed), the leadership team felt they needed to articulate the specific responsibilities and understand the "what, when, and how" aspects of the position.

The "when" was an easy answer: Now.

The "what" and the "how" are a bit more complex, but we can provide some generalizations of what the CDO should be focused on and how they should go about their role.

First, as I've said, the CDO needs to be a collaborator and communicator to help align the business and technology teams to a common vision for their data strategies and platforms, to drive digital transformation and meet business objectives.

In addition to the strategic vision, the CDO needs to work closely with the CIO to create and maintain a data-driven culture throughout the organization. This data-driven culture is an absolute requirement to support the changes brought on by digital transformation today and into the future.

"My role as a CDO has evolved to govern data, curate data, and convince subject matter experts that the data belongs to the business and not [individual] departments," Stu Gardos, CDO at Memorial Sloan Kettering Cancer Center, said at the CIO Perspectives conference.

Lastly, the CDO needs to work with the CIO and the IT team to implement proper data management and data governance systems and processes to ensure data is trustworthy, reliable, and available for analysis across the organization. That said, the CDO can't get bogged down in technology and systems but should keep their focus on the people and processes as it is their role to understand and drive the business value with the use of data.

In the meeting I mentioned earlier, I was asked what a successful CDO looks like. It's clear that a successful CDO crosses the divide between business and technology and institutes data as a trusted currency that is used to drive revenue and transform the business.

Ways a Chief Data Officer Drives Business Value

It is widely understood now that data drives business success. Data today is understood as a strategic asset – a critical ingredient for business innovation, and the currency for digital transformation. Data is now increasingly "owned" by business leaders, partnering with IT to realize the greatest value from their data. For many enterprises, this has led to a new role. The chief data officer (CDO) has been created as a bridge between business and IT.

The CDO role has tremendous potential, but many newly minted CDOs struggle to get started in a role that is often brand-new, both to them and to their business. They wonder how to build their new role into the enterprise and define their charter in a way that provides clear business value without alienating their peers. Based on Informatica's experience working with many successful

CDOs, I have put together the "Five Imperatives for the Chief Data Officer."

Imperatives for the Chief Data Officer

Most CDOs have to work through influence. They don't have the resources or authority to drive transformation by themselves and instead, must lead through collaboration and evangelism. Thus, as table stakes, CDOs need to understand their market, business objectives, and culture truly. While it is important to have a couple of quick wins, it is just as critical to building the relationships that will enable the CDO to be an effective leader. For a new CDO, the first 30 days should be focused on introduction and assessment, while removing any prior assumptions and perceptions; the next 30 are about planning.

In helping CDOs go from the chaos and dysfunction of scattered data silos to a holistic enterprise data environment, we have found a common path to success through these five imperatives:

1. Align the business and technology teams to a common data vision and strategy.

2. Identify compelling business drivers that are enabled by the data strategy.

3. Define a change management approach that builds a data-driven culture.

4. Develop a holistic roadmap and program that delivers incremental business value.

5. Leverage data governance to manage your data assets and establish shared accountability.

Fostering a Data-Driven Culture

This journey not only leads to a complete, integrated vision of your data strategy, but it also helps to foster a data-driven culture.

As many of our customers have told us, the biggest challenge of a digital transformation is not the technology — it is changing the people and processes in a meaningful, sustained way that prevents the technology from being underutilized or misused — or turning into shelf-ware.

Creating a Data-Driven Organization Depends on a Data-Driven Culture

Data Strategy and Business Intelligence aren't really about data; they're about the way data is used. The end goal isn't more silos, with a team that owns the data, the process, and its value. The end goal is a data-driven culture where everyone sees the value in data, understands the importance of collecting good data, has access to the data, and uses the data to support decision-making.

That culture is a total transformation of the way things work in many organizations, where the department owns data, or even the person, who collected it, and responsibility for making sure the data is good data lies with the person using it, not the person gathering it.

Creating that big of a transformation doesn't happen easily; you need to find ways to break through the silos and the barriers. Kelle O'Neal of First San Francisco Partners shared a five-step process to transform an organization's culture into a data-driven culture at the DATAVERSITY® Enterprise Data World 2016 Conference.

Data Is (Not) Just a Byproduct

One of O'Neal's key points is that:

"One of the things that is the biggest issue is getting people to change and getting people to think from a data-centric approach, and to think about data as a core part of their job regardless of whether they are the person at the front desk entering the visitors into the security system or whether they're a data analyst or they're the Chief Data Officer."

She pointed out that normally, "To the rest of your organization data is just a byproduct. They don't think about data as being so important." Employees work on doing their job function. Collecting data and ensuring that the collected data is quality data isn't a normal part of their job. It's not so much that they don't care about the data; it's that they don't even think about the data.

To make them care, there needs to be a compelling message that makes employees believe that it's important to be a data-driven culture.

Culture Exists in all Organizations

Every organization has a culture, and the cultural beliefs drive behaviors that affect the results you get. But changing culture is hard. O'Neal cited Dan Barnett and his concept of "Make or Break Culture." Barnett based his conclusion on experiments that were done at universities about decision making. They used MRI studies to see which parts of the brain were active during the decision-making process.

They found that gut decisions come from the limbic system, which is the animal part of the brain, the same place that decides "fight or flight." Higher-level decisions that take more analysis occur in the neocortex, the "human" part of the brain.

"The idea is that your decision-making process is taking some of the activity from your limbic system and communicating with your neocortex constantly. It's this integration between that animal part of your brain and the human part of your brain. It's the interaction between your belief system and your behaviors," O'Neal said.

As a result, that means that creating a data-driven culture requires creating both beliefs and behaviors that will then result in data-driven decisions. It's when the gut decisions and higher analysis both value the data that a company's employees truly care about data as a core part of their functioning. O'Neal went on,

"And so I want to be getting to the core part of what people believe about the data, about their company, about how the data and the company work together, and their role in that whole process."

Five-Step Framework Tackling Both Beliefs and Behavior

The framework O'Neal presented addresses both aspects of the culture. The first two steps, vision and purpose, address beliefs, and the last three steps, picture, plan, and participation affect behavior.

"Once you have all of this, then you can talk about the results, and you will be more able to achieve those results because you're driving the behaviors that you want," O'Neal said.

1. Vision: The vision is the desired future. It's an aspirational, motivational statement—a "big, hairy, audacious goal." The vision presents both the aspiration and the value of that aspiration to the future of the business. "If you can get them to believe the reason for the data and the data-driven culture, then you can more easily influence the behavior and get the results you want," O'Neal said.

2. Purpose: The purpose is the business reason to execute the vision. It explains the problem, what the evidence is, and what could happen if you don't act on that evidence.

3. Picture: The picture represents the future state. It's often best shown by comparing how things are now, the "before" state, with how they will be in the future. O'Neal explained its importance, saying

"The picture helps to drive behavior in two ways. It articulates what the future state should and will look like and then how are we going to get to that future state via guiding principles."

The guiding principles for the data-driven future should be tied back to the corporate vision and corporate values, plus any line of business guiding principles as well. The guiding principles articulate the organization's values and are the basis of decision-making and beliefs that drive behavior. O'Neale pointed out five characteristics a statement of principles needs to to be effective:

❖ a brief, clear statement of the concept

❖ applicable to the enterprise

❖ including an action verb

❖ clarifying the scope

❖ providing additional detail that explains why and how this picture is important.

4. Plan : The plan is a roadmap that helps people understand how the enterprise will get to that desired future state. It should detail the steps and timeline for implementing the necessary changes, including providing people with training and support to transition to the new way of doing things. The plan needs to make it clear for each, "what does this mean to me?" To do that, there might need to be multiple levels of plans, with an overarching roadmap for the enterprise and then group-specific roadmaps to apply the changes to each group.

5. Participation: Once the plan is clear, the last step of activating it and making it effective is defining participation, the way people engage and help execute the plan. One way of documenting participation is to use an operating model identifying roles and responsibilities. The objective is to make sure everyone knows what part they'll play in the future and how they'll get there. By focusing on this, you help people stop thinking about the past and start working towards the future.

Bringing It All Together

Summing it up, O'Neal said:

"The idea is that if you want to get the results you're looking for, then start at the top where you're thinking about things like your beliefs. Your vision statements and your purpose help people to believe and understand why data is important within the organization, and those beliefs will help them behave in a manner that delivers on that vision of becoming a data-driven culture."

By following these five steps to provide employees with clear communication about the objectives, the benefits of creating a data-driven culture, and the responsibilities of everyone to participate in that data-driven culture, companies can ease their transition and start building that new culture.

The Heartbeat Of A Data-Driven Culture

How To Create Commonly Understood Data

The whole world has fallen in love with the value that data can bring. The work that must be done to unlock that value is far less popular. As Thomas Edison said, "Opportunity is missed by most people because it is dressed in overalls and looks like work."

In the case of data, the fun stuff is playing with technology, distilling massive data sets using cool stuff like Hadoop, blending it together with systems like RedPoint or Alteryx, knitting it all together in Teradata, and then perhaps making a nifty chart or data discovery environment with technologies like Looker, Tableau or Qlik. Well, there is a lot of work in there, but it is an exciting to master a tool or discover something new.

The problem is that all across the world, such activities take place without first doing the work to determine the definition of the data going into the process. Where did this data come from? Is it the right data? Are we allowed to use this data? What other choices could we have made? How was it transformed? Are there any quality problems? And most important: Do we all understand this data in the same way?

All of these questions fall under the rubric of the snooze-inducing term data governance. If there was ever something that shows up dressed in overalls and looking like work, it is the activities needed to execute a program of data governance.

But let's say that we answer all the questions listed above: How much more powerful does data become? How does it change the relationship between people and data in business?

The Pitfalls of Ungoverned Data

In my view, using ungoverned data isn't the worst case—using no data is worse. But data that doesn't have a clear definition as shown in Figure 1 leads to two situations, neither of which is good.

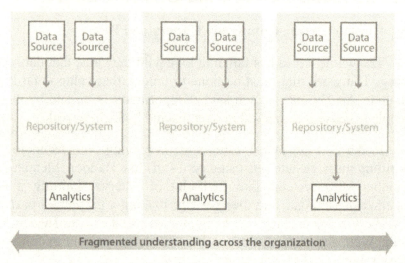

Figure 1. The World Without Data Governance

The first is the Data Rorschach Effect, which happens when people look at data and just see whatever they want to see. If everyone in the company is looking at their dashboard created to be just the way they want it, there is no way for a consistent big picture to be assembled. The definition of the customer in one report may be completely different than the customer in another. Same goes for revenue and expenses. Furthermore, everyone may have a different model of what drives growth. If data is not defined, it can be a springboard for free association, often self-serving free-association.

The second situation is the Data Brawl, which occurs when someone uses data to draw a conclusion that is damaging to someone else in the company. The CFO says that sales are dropping because she is only counting closed deals. The VP of sales says sales are rising because there are a record number of deals in contract negotiations. The first response by the injured party is usually to attack the quality of the data. This then leads to an acrimonious battle which good data governance would have avoided.

How to Implement Data Governance

I feel about data governance just as Marianne Moore said of poetry, "I too dislike it." But as Moore noted in her poem, "one discovers in it, after all, a place for the genuine." To me, data governance is all the work that must take place to make data into poetry, something that is distilled, compact, and radiating with meaning. I may dislike the work, but, as Moore does, I love the result.

There are many roads to data governance, but I recently came across a company, Collibra, that is taking an approach that has a strong chance of working in many companies. As I have in past stories, we are going to look at the essential idea of data governance by examining the approach that a vendor, in this case, Collibra, is taking to solving the problem.

If you look up what management consultants and lots of other experts have written about data governance, you will get a lot of complex gobbledygook about ornate processes. Data governance can be complex, but to me the fundamental ideas are simple. The goals of data governance include:

Truth: Create an agreed upon, commonly understood, searchable, integrated model, definitions, and catalog of the data that describes a business.

Communication: Document the model and definitions in all its forms so that people using data can conveniently know what a particular field or set of data means.

Change: Implement a process that allows the model and definitions to evolve and grow through a team-based process in which everyone plays the appropriate role.

Convenience: Integrate and automate related processes for data quality, granting access, updating databases schemas, publishing metadata, and so on to achieve these goals.

I think the experience of Warby Parker, the innovative eyeglass retailer, shows this quite well. Lon Binder, the CTO of Warby Parker, and Carl Anderson, the director of analytics who recently published Creating a Data-Driven Organization, implemented a streamlined approach to data governance in the following way:

❖ The data describing the company's operations was landed in a SQL data warehouse.

❖ The analytics team analyzed all the concepts used by the business staff and analysts at the company, which were mostly embedded in spreadsheets.

❖ A new set of definitions for the various types of customers and revenue and so forth were implemented using Looker, which allowed analysts to dive into the data easily and summarize it and explore it using pivot tables.

❖ The definitions were documented in a GitHub Git Book repository, which was used as an integrated catalog of all the data at Warby Parker.

The result was a simple and highly functional data governance process that works for a mid-sized, but data-obsessed organization. More can be found in these stories that refer to Warby Parker ("Why You Can't Be Data-driven Without A Data Catalog" and "Why Digital Paper Is Killing Efficiency and How To Stop It.")

How Collibra Delivers Data Governance at Scale

So now imagine that you have a team of hundreds or thousands of people using data scattered all over dozens of major applications and data warehouse and analytics system. You don't have a data warehouse anymore; you have a data supply chain. Customer data may be in 10 different places. Even if you have a master data management system to collect all of the master data and make sense of it, you still have the challenge of managing the process of agreeing on the basic concepts.

In such an environment you will always have a heterogeneous set of applications and data analytics repositories. The idea of one repository to rule them all where the governance will happen is a fantasy.

Also, you will have data that is owned by different parts of the organization, and that will need agreements about how data is shared and the service levels that describe how data will be maintained.

This is the world that Collibra is focused on. The software is constructed and used based on the following assumptions:

- ❖ The integrated catalog is going to start small and grow and change at a rapid pace.

- ❖ You need a process for managing the evolution and expansion of this catalog and communicating about the changes; tribal knowledge will no longer work.

- ❖ The management of the integrated catalog must embrace a heterogeneous implementation and use of the catalog and definitions by many different types of tools.

- ❖ Automation of this process will not be complete, but will gradually grow as mechanisms of integration mature.

The Role of the Integrated Catalog in Data Governance

Figure 2. The Role of the Integrated Catalog in Data Governance

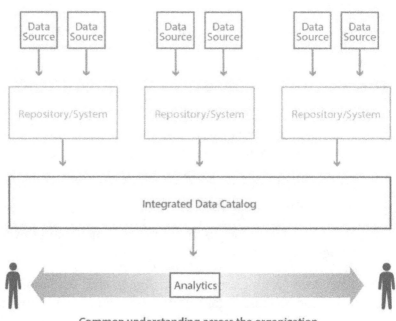

Common understanding across the organization

Collibra CEO Felix Van de Maele, who co-founded the company based on research done in graduate school, realized that data governance is a process that is never truly complete. It must be supported as a moving vector, not as an end state. "Our goal is just to find somewhere to start at a customer, to find an important data set that needs to be trusted and understood in the same way across the business," he says. "Once we show what we can do, the data-obsessed in the company arrive and want help in making their data a shared asset, and adoption just blossoms from there."

Implementation of the Collibra vision shown in Figure 3 is based the following principles:

* ❖ The integrated catalog and definitions are independent of any implementation technology.

❖ The catalog is searchable to allow analysts to find governed and approved data available to them.

❖ During construction of the catalog, auto-discovery is used wherever possible to import implementation layer data and metadata.

❖ The business-focused integrated catalog is created and connected to the logical and physical model through a process of design, construction of standards and policies, and formal approval, all controlled by workflows.

❖ A ticket-based process is used for addressing problems and changes.

❖ Integration is supported with a variety of implementation technologies to perform various data governance related tasks:

❖ Harvesting of the physical layer and other intermediate data models from databases and programs like Erwin.

❖ Delivery of metadata describing lineage of fields to analysis technology like Tableau.

❖ Automatic creation of new fields in databases based on updates of the catalog.

❖ Certification of the output of reports and analytics systems as based on accurate and approved data.

❖ Integration with data quality tools to report on the quality of the data and efforts to improve quality.

❖ Other integrations are frequently added as part of the Collibra Connect part of the product.

Collibra Product Capabilities for Implementing Data Governance

When companies use Collibra to implement a data governance process and create a shareable, commonly understood data catalog, they take an incremental approach:

- ❖ First, a high-value report or dashboard becomes the focus.

- ❖ Pre-existing data definitions are imported into Collibra.

- ❖ The physical data models are imported into Collibra.

- ❖ The team who is going to construct the catalog is defined and assigned roles inside Collibra

- ❖ The tasks to create the catalog are assigned to the team and proceed through a defined workflow.

- ❖ Tasks include the creation of concepts and definitions at a business level, the creation of the logical and physical data models, documentation, integration with varying levels of technology for modeling and data quality, and approval.

- ❖ The result is a business level catalog that is connected as much as it can be to all of the mechanisms for using data, monitoring it, and ensuring data quality.

Figure 3. Collibra Product Capabilities for Implementing Data Governance

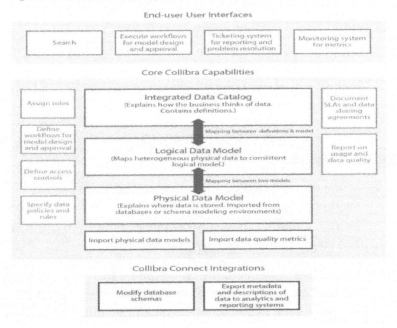

This process is then repeated over and over again to gradually build out a comprehensive catalog of the crucial data in a company.

Collibra's vision has a variety of advantages:

❖ The catalog in Collibra assumes a heterogeneous storage of data in many technologies. Many other technologies of this sort assume that one repository or technology will be used as the center, which limits the scope of data that can be governed.

❖ Collibra puts as much focus on the process of creating, updating, communicating about, and using the data catalog as it does on the catalog itself. The to-do list for all the work of data governance is managed, not just the catalog.

❖ Collibra doesn't rely on pervasive automation. In other words, you can notice problems and assign people to fix them in other systems.

❖ Collibra is useful without the Collibra Connect integrations with other technologies but becomes more powerful as more integrations show up. The integrations provide something extra such as reporting on data quality, adding metadata to analytics tools, or the ability update a schema in a database by updating the catalog but do not get in the way of the core value created.

The biggest worry I have about Collibra is how to motivate people to participate.

❖ When the data catalog is complete, it becomes very useful to analysts who want to find high-quality data, but there is energy required to build enough definitions so that it becomes a benefit to analysts.

❖ Lots of the benefits of the commonly understood, integrated catalog are only clear after you have suffered from not having agreement on what the data in your company means. Do people have to suffer first to understand the value of Collibra and a commonly understood data catalog?

❖ The work to create and maintain the catalog is substantial at first and not trivial as the catalog grows. How do companies recognize in KPIs and MBOs that this is important work for everyone, not just for the data governance team?

The crucial challenge facing companies today concerning data is not how they will address the fun parts. The fancy toys will be bought because they are exciting. The companies that make the most of the data they spend so much to collect will be the ones that have enthusiasm for the overall-clad work of data governance that is, turning raw and messy data into something genuine and meaningful like poetry. When that occurs, changes in data lead to changes in action, not to confusion.

CREATING A DATA CULTURE

The chief data officers can take these steps to build a culture around the information that's at the heart of today's business.

Young companies often have an inherent advantage over their long-standing competitors: They were born from data. Their businesses are based on metrics and interrelated facts. Sharing data is part of their DNA.

Traditional companies view data differently. Born offline, they see data as a tool to run their businesses, not drive their strategy. They prize experience and intuition over data-based decision-making.

The differences are stark, and so are the results. Companies that rate themselves ahead of their peers in their use of data are three times more likely to rate their financial performance as more advanced, according to research by the Economist Intelligence Unit.

Chief data officers (CDOs) can close the gap. Charged with developing a strategy for data and managing their organization's data ecosystem, CDOs are responsible for educating employees about the power and possibilities of data. By instilling values around data, they can reshape their organization's use of it.

Data cultures are becoming pivotal as organizations develop more progressive digital business strategies and apply meaning to big data. As companies become more adept at managing the trail of clicks, swipes, and comments that create the unique virtual identities we call Code Halos; a data culture helps put the digital code to smart use in building more clairvoyant and frictionless user experiences.

The following steps will help guide CDOs to create successful, thriving data cultures:

1. Map your organization's data supply chain.

2. Focus on the "art of the possible."

3. Be transparent about data.

4. Develop reward-sharing mechanisms.

5. Identify areas of friction within the organization

6. Elevate the conversation to focus on strategy and innovation.

The stakes are high. Without a shift in culture and attitude toward data, traditional organizations are at risk of failing to realize a return on their investments in sound data architecture and infrastructure.

Data Culture: The Missing Link in Your Data Strategy?

No matter how smartly crafted, a data strategy is incomplete without a data-oriented culture to support it. Data culture and data success are intertwined and interdependent. Organizations can't have one without the other.

No matter how smartly crafted, a data strategy is incomplete without a data-oriented culture to support it. Data culture and data success are intertwined and interdependent.

A data-driven culture is a workplace environment that employs a consistent, repeatable approach to tactical and strategic decision-making through emphatic and empirical data proof. Put simply; it's an organization that bases decisions on data, not gut instinct.

While intuition has its place, the wide availability of analytics has elevated objective decision-making to the new standard, and it's the CDO's responsibility to help the organizations embrace it.

The shift can be complex, requiring departments and functions to replace longstanding processes with new ways of working. The first step involves priming the organization for change. We recommend a three-pronged approach to guide objective decision-making: Encourage employee use of data; engage with employees on the possibilities of data, and educate them on how to manipulate and use data.

Take a Cue from Employees

Technology executives spend most of their waking hours considering data in all its forms; to them, it's the language of business. But too many employees, data remains in the purview of those who understand coding and APIs. To them, data is strictly for geek nation.

Encourage, Engage and Educate

Integrating data into your organization's daily operations is no easy task. We recommend setting the stage for data's expanded role with a three-pronged approach that encourages, engages and educates. Before meaningful outcomes can be produced, the benefits of a data culture need to be communicated, as well as the downside of not changing.

Encourage: Encouraging a data culture is akin to developing a business case. Like all effective businesses cases, this one is a part value proposition, part salesmanship. The CDO's job is to convince the organization of data's importance in workplace decisions. Pointing out data's omnipresence can help connect the dots.

For example, most employees are already adept at making data-driven decisions outside the office. Before making important financial decisions such as buying a home, most will evaluate their income, expenses and other factors. Supportive data can similarly help with making smarter workplace decisions, and it's the CDO's job to show them how.

Engage: An atmosphere of experimentation is important, as some data initiatives will succeed, while others will fail. The message should be that all ideas are welcome.

Once constituents begin to link data to decision-making, the CDO will need to engage them by demonstrating how new combinations of data can uncover new insights. The idea is to get organizations excited about data and what it can achieve. Explore new combinations of data and tap into new data sources, both internal and external.

Educate: Training needs to occur across areas such as data management and integration, business intelligence, dashboards, and visualization. Without such training in relevant tools, techniques and technologies, exploration and inquisitiveness will grind to a halt. Enlist IT supports to train internal and external constituents — team members, peers, consumers of data — in how to use, manipulate, play with and interpret data to make decisions and derive insights.

Bridging this gap is necessary for establishing a data culture, as CDOs need all hands on deck. By reframing data as information, and the data culture as one in which all employees can — and should — participate, CDOs can begin to demystify data and build a more inclusive foundation that resonates with employees at all levels.

By reframing data as information, and the data culture as one in which all employees can — and should — participate, CDOs can begin to demystify data.

Many employees are already familiar with the collaborative consumption that makes data cultures tick. As consumers, they are part of the welcoming customer base that has greeted the sharing economy and propelled businesses such as Airbnb and Uber to multi-billion-dollar valuations.

They understand the benefits of sharing both data and underutilized capacity

— literally and figuratively — and they are likely ready to step into their workplace roles as data allies.

Much of the effort involved in getting them there begins in the CDO's office. While the role of the CDO still varies widely (see sidebar below), the development of a data culture always starts here.

Establishing a more fluid role for data within traditional organizations is indeed possible. Sectors such as government and education, which are striving to become more data-driven as part of the open-data movement, have notched some early wins.

Getting a Jump on Business: Where Data Cultures Are Already Succeeding

Corporations aren't alone in their efforts to establish a data culture. Municipalities and educational institutions are also striving to develop transparency, collaboration and innovation around their data — and gaining some surprising results.

Spurred by the open-data movement, cities around the globe have thrown open their data stores to citizens and businesses. Singapore, Copenhagen, and London are among the municipalities sharing data, with the goal of improving public policy and services. In the U.S., Philadelphia recently took the wraps off a portal that brims with access to more than 250 local data sets, applications and APIs.

The results are leading to a raft of new services. Helsinki, Finland, for instance, developed a mobile app that blends GPS capabilities with city data to guide blind individuals through the city using voice commands.

States are also getting in on the action. A coding contest hosted by Colorado inspired the development of Beagle Score, a widget that integrates with online commercial real estate listings and rates business locations by variables such as taxes and zoning.18 To create Beagle Score, its creators mashed up information from 30 state-offered data sets.

The education sector is also looking to establish a more fluid role for data within its traditional boundaries. St. Petersburg College in Florida credits its improved student experience with a flourishing data culture.19 Kentucky's Department of education opened a dialog to make information more usable when it found that its massive data warehouse was too unwieldy for teachers and administrators to use. The state points to the collaborative effort as the source of its increased high school graduation and postsecondary enrollment rates.

Steps to Better Manage Data as an Asset

With the following steps, your organization can begin to reshape its attitude toward data and manage data as a strategic asset.

Map your organization's use of data

Departmental silos of information are the nemesis of thriving data cultures. To promote the view of data as a flexible asset that's usable by multiple departments, organizations need to educate employees on how the data they use daily ripples through other parts of the organization. Employees need to see the big picture.

Mapping your organization's data supply chain is a useful tool for gaining that 30,000-foot view. For CDOs, it's an essential step. The map tracks each data set's path through the organization. Who creates the data? Who consumes it? What decisions do they make with it? Who stores it? Who might be abusing it? Maps can be drawn from data sets that are used by individuals or groups, and then linked back to business processes.

The data supply chain map becomes a framework to which everyone within the organization can refer. It provides context for how data is used and how employees' data usage fits into the broader enterprise.

Data maps can also uncover "dark data," or pockets of information that go largely unstudied, such as machine data and customer service call logs. Dark data is typically difficult to integrate and analyze due to technical issues such as formatting, variety, and velocity.

Dark data can benefit organizations in several ways. For example, reviewing machine logs from dispensing units with geolocation data can help predict inventory patterns and improve ordering processing to avoid loss of revenue. One insurance provider improved its fraud detection by 30% and reduced claims expenses approximately 3% by combining its historical claims data with syndicated data — from credit bureaus, hospitals, auto OEMs and police records — to reveal patterns of fraud and fraud indicators.

Be transparent about data

Data becomes an asset only if its accuracy is trusted, its provenance is well established, and its security is safeguarded. But data also requires openness, even as it is protected from fraudsters and kept private for regulatory reasons.

The CDO organization can build trust in data by tracking its quality and lineage and providing multiple use cases — including examples in which a data set should not be used.

Transparency extends even to data with accuracy issues. When confidence in data quality is low, or the data's lineage cannot be established, the CDO organization can enhance the data's value with suggestions for specific uses.

Consider a data set on customer spend, for example. High data sparsity regarding attributes such as date of birth or address may render the data unusable for personalized offers, where laser-like precision is required. But the data set is still relevant for insights that can be drawn with broader strokes, such as understanding segment-based spending habits.

Focus on the "art of the possible"

Awareness of data's flexibility is the hallmark of any data culture. It leads to what we call the "art of the possible" — that is, a knack for spotting alternative uses for data.

For employees, understanding data's versatility means acquiring new habits. For instance, departments and functions regularly encounter data for which they may have no use when looked at through the lens of their line of business. In most companies, the data is then forgotten or discarded. By viewing the same information within the context of a data map, however, other uses for the data emerge, such as links to upstream and downstream consumers. The data's potential to create new insights, and in some cases alternate paradigms for business strategies, becomes apparent.

Consider ways your organization can find alternative or unusual uses for the data it creates. By encouraging employees to identify other departments or teams that can benefit from data, your organization promotes and invests in its data culture.

Focusing on the art of the possible can lead to the corporate nirvana of data monetization. Netflix, for example, devised its Emmy-winning hit show House of Cards by gathering routine viewer data and carefully correlating it in new ways. The streaming service discovered that subscribers who watched the original BBC series of the same name were also avid consumers of movies starring actor Kevin Spacey or directed by David Fincher. When Netflix licensed the BBC series for a remake, it signed Spacey to star and Fincher to direct. It's a perfect example of what I call Code Halo thinking — and the rest, as they say, is viewing history.

Develop reward-sharing mechanisms

Sharing data successes and celebrating the individuals and teams behind them is essential to promoting a healthy data culture. To help spread the word, organizations need a communications strategy for recognizing such success.

Recognition can occur in many forms, including videos, blogs and special occasion gatherings, such as luncheons. Setting up a company portal to highlight data successes is another option. Rewards and recognition for data initiatives should also be included in formal corporate excellence programs.

Celebrated data initiatives should be aligned with the organization's innovation objectives. Does your organization want to differentiate itself by understanding its customers in new ways? By penetrating new markets? The data initiatives should support those efforts and reward the ones that advance them. For example, a telecom carrier whose goals include reducing customer churn might reward a team that identifies data that leads to insights into how to predict customers' potential to defect.

Identify Areas Of Friction Within The Organization

Creating a data culture hinges on a thorough understanding of how the departments within your company function — and where there are disconnect and contradiction.

A thriving data culture depends on an environment in which everyone can share information without being perceived as negative. For example, tension often exists between product engineering and sales. Engineering's objective is to freeze requirements so it can get products to market on time and within budget; for sales to meet its goal of boosting revenues, however, it prefers a more fluid approach to requirements in which it can funnel requests for additional features to engineering as it learns about them through customer discussions.

Data gives the two departments common ground. By using data to prioritize features, teams can objectively choose between time to market and cost. For example, what does customer feedback reveal about feature preferences and customer satisfaction levels? Data improves collaboration by keeping the departmental focus on facts, not emotions.

Elevate The Conversation To Emphasize Strategy And Innovation

A data culture offers many positive benefits, such as greater employee engagement and higher productivity. But its real purpose is to sharpen corporate strategy and drive innovation. Openly discussing strategies and innovation goals provide employees with a clear view of data's role in the company's overall mission and reinforce their connection to the larger organization.

Traditional business models often fail to make that link. Employees can be reluctant to share data because they don't perceive the value of data they create or are unable to connect it to organizational objectives. Self-preservation can also fuel a reluctance to share, as employees are often defined by the expertise they bring to the table.

Promoting a deeper understanding of the organization's big picture can inspire more prolific sharing by employees and foster a sense of belonging. Bringing employees together for events such as enterprise-level ideation sessions and hackathons can help accelerate strategy and innovation efforts. Appliance-maker Whirlpool attributes most of its innovations to structured ideation sessions,24 and Facebook has famously hosted monthly hackathons during which employees could work on projects unrelated to work.25 In January 2015, British Airways gathered writers, designers, entrepreneurs, and programmers to find ways to enhance flight arrivals.

Greater transparency regarding strategy and innovation also prepares your organization for the data culture — and workforce — of the future. By 2025, millennials will account for as much as 75% of the workforce, and their values are expected to create profound shifts in corporate goals. For example, two-thirds of millennials would prefer to earn $40,000 a year at a job they love rather than $100,000 a year at a job they think is boring, according to a 2014 survey.28 Retaining their loyalty within the data culture is key.

Looking Ahead

Transitioning to a data culture is a challenge that requires dramatic change for traditional organizations, but the first steps toward that end can be simple ones. Even if your organization isn't yet ready to launch a full data-culture program, it can begin to lay the foundation. Start by identifying employees who can serve as data ambassadors within your organization's data-driven culture. Employees who believe in the power of data are key allies for successful CDOs. In the words of Facebook's Mark Zuckerberg, "A trusted referral influences people more than the best broadcast message."

With your data allies identified, consider executing the first of our six steps as a pilot project. Mapping your organization's data supply chain will potentially launch your organization toward managing data as a strategic asset.

DECIDING TO HIRE A CDO

If all of this has made you think that your own company could benefit from having a CDO, then here are some important things to consider before you proceed with the hiring process.

Know Why You Want One

The skill set required to be a CDO is a rare one, and the paths to becoming a qualified candidate for the CDO role can vary quite a bit. To avoid wasting time in your hiring process, it's best to start by taking time to outline the particular needs your organization has around data.

Some questions you should ask of your key business stakeholders include:

❖ Are you part of a regulated industry or are there professional data standards that will make compliance and data governance your highest priority?

❖ Do you need to reorganize your data and your focus from being product-centric to customer-centric?

❖ Are you missing opportunities to add products or services to your offerings, which could be illuminated by internal or external data?

❖ Could your current processes and outcomes be optimized even further by better analytics?

❖ Are there data-derived insights in one part of your organization that could benefit other divisions if those insights were shared?

❖ Is there a need for increased transparency into your data, or a good reason to publish your data publicly in open datasets?

Once you've identified your primary reason for hiring a CDO, then it's time to start thinking about the rewards of having one and describing a set of use cases that will get others excited about these possibilities.

"You have to generate demand for the role before you hire a some- body and get them to do the work," said Charles Thomas of Wells Fargo. "People need to believe that we do need to look at the customer end-to-end. If you don't do that, the CDO spends their first year or two justifying why they're there."

Develop a list of use cases where the ability to use data to generate new insights or products could improve the way you do business— and the way other stakeholders could perform in their roles. Then the CDO you put in place won't have to spend as much time on overall evangelism and will be able to hit the ground running on projects that will directly generate business value as soon as they arrive.

Look for the Right Skill Set

Today's CDOs come from many different backgrounds: some were engineers who had the business mindset required to move into the role, while others were business people who had a keen awareness of technology and the soft skills to work with other technologists to get the job done. Still, others came from a legal or humanities background, with the communication and persuasion skills to achieve culture change. Which set of skills should run deepest in your own CDO depends in part on what you need them to accomplish.

Technology chops

It can't be said enough that a data-driven enterprise is about creating more value for the business, rather than focusing on technology for technology's sake. Still, there's no getting around the fact that extracting insights from data requires a deeply technical skill set. Many people believe that the ability to navigate the tools and techniques of working with data is the most critical skill a CDO can have.

"I think data engineering is what defines this role," said Azarias Reda, formerly of the RNC, when you are "building products that depend on or that benefit from the data that you have collected."

Of course, the CDO may not be building projects directly. Often, they are overseeing a team of data scientists and engineers or facilitating that work inside various departments of the organization. But Amy Gershkoff of Zynga described how important her technical skills are to managing her team: "Because I can have conversations at that technical level, it enables me to ensure that my team is producing the best work. It also enables me to be a sounding board for my team when they get stuck, or when they have challenges in solving a particularly difficult modeling problem or data science problem."

At the very least, a CDO needs to have enough technical savvy to understand what is possible to accomplish with data—and what the limits of data are, too.

Business thinking

The ability to speak knowledgeably about the specifics of working with data is an important skill for the CDO. But the way Anthony Algmin, former CDO of the Chicago Transit Authority and currently the CDO of Uturn Data Solutions, sees it, the real issue is a focus on business and strategic thinking.

"The problem isn't that we have CIOs, Chief Data Officers, and Chief Technology Officers—they are all meaningful," said Algmin. "The real problem is that the first time a person coming up in an IT organization is asked to be strategic is when they are given one of these C-level roles."

We need to shift the way we train data engineers and data scientists and bring them up to the organization, giving them opportunities to learn all aspects of the business and practice strategic thinking from much earlier on in their careers. Doing so will create a much larger pool of hiring candidates for the CDO down the road. But in the meantime, CDOs must have the ability to think strategically about what the business needs and how to use data to meet those objectives.

"Every business has to be getting better at what they do by using data," said Algmin. "Because if they aren't, their competitors are, and their competitors will win."

There are also times when industry expertise in the CDO can be very helpful. If you're looking to answer important questions about your competitive landscape, for example, then you may need someone with a deep domain knowledge who can help ensure that you're formulating the right questions. The insights data yields are only as good as the questions you ask of it, and that's the core advantage that business thinking brings.

Political skills

Finally, while the ability to work well with others is a "nice to have" characteristic for any employee, the importance of diplomacy and people skills to the role of the CDO can't be overstated.

"Of the many attributes, you need a chief data officer with the political savvy and leadership qualities who can bring people together," said Barbara Cohn, former CDO of New York State. "In every position that I have held, that's been the key to success. It's about the people and the partnerships."

Several CDOs described investing a lot of time in talking to others inside their organization, listening for their colleagues' pain points, and then deliberately making connections between the data strategy of the organization as a whole and the individual problems departments were facing to both bring people on board and accomplish their own goals.

"People are risk averse, and new ideas are a culture change," said Cohn. "It takes time, but you need to build those relationships. It must be a true collaboration. Once you have that trust factor and respect, you can move the agenda, and anything is possible."

A CDO also needs to be diplomatic enough to manage competing priorities. "So much of being a CDO is prioritizing decision-making and getting decisions made by an organization," Jennifer Ippoliti, formerly of Raymond James, explained. "The CDO often is a person who ends up having to say 'no' to a lot of people: 'No, we can't address your issue until next year or the year after.' And that needs to be done in a way that is not going to make a lot of enemies."

Micheline Casey, formerly of the Federal Reserve Board, agrees. "Whether you're talking about the business side of the house or the tech side of the house, the CDO is balancing a lot of often conflicting priorities and needs across the organization." She said, "so the ability to communicate well to everyone, from senior business executives down to the technical staff on a day-to-day basis, is another really important aspect of this role."

Not only is the art of diplomacy helpful to the task of prioritization, but the art of influence is also critical to the task of evangelization. "You are a cultural change agent more than you are a technologist," said Algmin. "So it is about influencing people. It is about convincing groups to get on board. Welcome to being an executive."

Executive-level experience

To find a hiring prospect with an equal mix of technical, business, and political skills is a tall enough order. To find a prospect who has all of that plus the requisite experience to work at the executive level is very difficult indeed.

"In my mind, a true CDO is a seasoned executive that has built up very deep knowledge of data and how to apply that data. And that is something that takes 15 to 20 years," said Mark Ramsey, formerly of Samsung. "It is very similar to if you are looking for a chief financial officer for an organization. A true CDO is going to have that level of acumen from data and an analytics perspective."

It may be tempting to sacrifice this criterion before the others, because some of the other skills—particularly those related to data science and analytics—may be more abundant in graduates of newer programs. But don't underestimate the importance of both career experience and gravitas.

"Data is the lifeblood of any organization," said Algmin, "and it is the closest thing to measurable knowledge about an organization that you can find. And if you entrust something that important to somebody who is not an important role, then what are you saying about your business?"

How can aspiring CDOs get this experience? And what career trajectory should a hiring committee look for in a CDO, then? "Don't think of your career—your aspirations—as a ladder," said Ursula Cottone of Citizen's Bank. "Climbing a ladder will have you be in a particular space, but you are not going to get the breadth. I like to use the term 'lattice' or 'climbing wall,' because you often have to go sideways to go up."

Hunting Unicorns

While these four individual criteria—technology chops, business thinking, political skills, and executive-level experience— are each important in their right, the real merit lies at the intersections between them. For example, because every CDO will rely not only on their background and experience but also the skills and experience of stakeholders across the company, every CDO needs to be "bilingual," able to speak knowledgeably about both technology and business.

"Being able to bridge the language of business and the language of data and technology, and being able to translate between those two, is the critical skill set," said Scott Kaylie, formerly of QuestPoint.

"And I think typically that's going to be someone who is strong in one, and they can understand the other." Not only the ability to understand the other, but also the innate curiosity that drives someone to ask questions and to learn, will be a truly significant asset.

Because it's these intersections that are so important, it's difficult to say which of the skills can be de-emphasized in favor of the others. Certainly, some can be learned on the job or made up for by hiring the right mix of team members. Ultimately, however, they must all be present for the CDO to be effective.

"I would say all of those are critically important: technical skills, business and strategic thinking, people management skills, good communication skills, and collaboration skills," said Amy Gershkoff of Zynga. "It is all of those things together that make a good CDO, and I would say no one of those skills is more important than any other because they are all so very critical."

In other words: the ideal candidate has a mix of technical chops and business savvy, with the political skills to work well with others in all parts of the organization and the requisite experience to work at the executive level. If this sounds a little bit like a mythical creature to you, well, you're not far off.

"It's almost like you have to be a magician," said Tyrone Grandison, Deputy CDO of the federal Department of Commerce. "You are supposed to be doing so many things from vetting the products, evangelizing, communicating to executives both outside and inside the organization, and setting the strategic direction where everything should be going. You can't do all that by yourself in a regular work week.

THE CHALLENGES OF THE CDO

W hen your role is nascent and evolving, there are many inherent challenges, to be sure. But add that lack of stability and established expectations to a role that must keep up with a rapidly shifting technological landscape while simultaneously navigating the politics of many divisions and departments, and you've got one very tall order.

Technical Challenges

When it comes to supporting the most critical business goals, internal data is almost never enough by itself. So in addition to gathering the company's data, the CDO may also be gathering external data from open APIs, vendors, or other sources, and making it all work together to answer the questions that matter to the business. Jennifer Ippoliti, former CDO of Raymond James Financial, sees this as one of the significant challenges of the role.

"The biggest challenge is how to deliver on these grand visions that people have of what you can do with data management," she said, "when your actual data is still sitting in silos, and not consistent, and not using standard definitions, and standard field formats, and so on." This challenge boils down to two crucial words: data quality.

Data accuracy

Data quality includes multiple considerations, such as latency and completeness. But in the quest for faster and bigger data, many people take data accuracy for granted. Said Senior and Retired President and CEO of Blue Cross Life Insurance Company of Canada James Gilligan, "I don't think organizations naturally think of data quality —you think of data coming in, and you move it along, and you take for granted that it's correct."

Like many companies, Blue Cross Life Insurance Company of Canada relies on data from a partner organization that it does not itself collect or standardize. Sometimes they receive data that is obviously inaccurate, and it is very tempting for their experts to attempt to make the necessary corrections to be able to put it to use. "But right away as soon as you do that," said Gilligan, "you've got two problems: 1) the data are wrong, and 2) you've got a new source of truth. Presumably, other people are using that same data for other things. So even on a small-scale business with a lot of this kind of activity, the stakes are very high."

Not only is there a lot of risk in creating a new source of truth and diverging from the data others may be using, but it can also be a significant drain on resources. "In a lot of places," said Gilligan, "the people who are doing the clean-up are highly paid people who were hired to do other things, but they can't do it until the data is clean.

Some of this janitorial work can't be helped. But when highly skilled analysts face the prospect of cleaning up outside data on a regular basis, the evangelization skills of the CDO can make a difference. "The evangelization is particularly poignant for any organization that relies on receiving data from an external source," said Gilligan, "because you have to evangelize the normative expectations for data quality and make sure those expectations are understood and carried forward by those who are outside your organization."

On the most cutting edge, these types of data quality headaches are becoming less of an issue. Expert data scientists like Claudia Perlich can do very nuanced analyses with fairly noisy data. At the 2015 Strata + Hadoop World conference in New York, Perlich gave a talk titled, "Death of the click: How big data is killing your favorite metrics." In which she discussed how many traditional metrics and KPIs such as the cherished click-through rate (CTR) are diminishing in value as new and more sophisticated techniques become possible.

"When what we were doing was reporting in aggregation," said John Akred, CTO and co-founder of Silicon Valley Data Science, a consulting firm, "the most complicated thing was maintaining moving averages: then the 'garbage in, garbage out' thing makes sense because the input and output are intimately related. But now we need to rethink data in the enterprise," because of the techniques that Perlich and others are developing. At the same time, most organizations aren't there yet. As science fiction author William Gibson famously wrote: "The future is already here—it's just not very evenly distributed."

Data context

Sometimes, data quality means both accuracy and something more: context. For organizations and governments that make their data open, the inherent expectation of that type of data quality adds pressure.

"No question about it," said Barbara Cohn, former CDO of New York State. "The relevance, the timeliness, consistency, reliability, and accuracy—it's an expectation of the public, as well as the government. But it is not achieved serendipitously. It takes a lot of work."

Cohn was brought in to be the first CDO of New York State by Governor Andrew Cuomo, who showed a deep understanding of the importance of data. He consolidated the IT divisions of the various state agencies under one umbrella, the Office of Information Technology Services, or ITS, to improve transparency and access to data across agencies. It began developing and publishing a series of rigorously curated datasets, a library that now includes more than 1400 datasets about everything from winning lottery numbers since 1980 to a map of solid waste management facilities across the state. These datasets are available not only inter-agency but also publicly. Cohn's team made sure each one had extensive metadata and overview documents to make it as thorough and useful as possible.

"Once you are on the Internet, people forget, you are global immediately," said Cohn. "And we wanted people, no matter where they are accessing our data—whether in New York State, California, Africa, Europe, or anywhere in the world—we wanted to ensure maximum understanding by enriching content with context to maximize business value and insight, and inspire innovation and cooperative problem-solving."

How does one ensure maximum value? "It is all about the utility and reuse of the data," said Cohn. "If it is not quality data, it is not going to have value."

Legacy systems

Another common technical challenge occurs when companies merge, acquire, IPO, or otherwise, reorganize in ways that affect their legacy infrastructure. Said Gilligan, "When you have M&A, you end up with multiple systems, and it's not just a technical challenge about merging the systems—the more important issue is how you merge the data? Because probably the data will be configured differently. Is a client a client, or is a client a customer, or is a customer a group? It's a huge problem."

It can be tempting to rebuild systems from the ground up. "The natural tendency of people is to think, 'It's probably better to start over,' so we'll clear the decks and start from scratch," said Gilligan. "And that might be the worst thing to do because you'll lose a lot of richness from that legacy data." But retaining that institutional knowledge can mean huge amounts of labor to overhaul systems and standards.

The technological aspects of working with data offer many real challenges. Ultimately, however, the biggest challenges lie elsewhere. Even when it comes to data quality, as Citizen's Bank CDO Ursula Cottone points out, "Technology can't fix data quality problems. It can highlight them, but it can't fix them."

Business Challenges

Much can be done with data, as the press delight in showing us every day, but the key is to do things with data that will directly support business objectives. The CDO is in charge, in large part, of making sure that the paths an organization pursues with data are pursued the right reasons: business reasons.

"Data, while supported by technology, is not fundamentally a technology problem. Your information systems can house the data, but your questions—like, 'Should we be running this program?'— those are business questions," said Joy Bonaguro of San Francisco. "And technology can help you manage them, but if you don't have good business questions, it doesn't matter what kind of technology you have."

Eugene Kolker, former CDO of Seattle Children's Hospital, agreed: "We're trying to improve business; we're trying to bring better service to our customers. It's better to start from that angle than to start from the technology. And in our case, our customers are families with sick children, which makes it all the more imperative that we give our absolute best!"

On data strategy

To develop good business questions and to answer them in ways that create significant value, there must be a sound data strategy in place. The ideal data strategy is written in collaboration with both the business stakeholders and the technological stakeholders, so it is well understood and agreed upon by everyone involved. It outlines the objectives that matter most to the company, lays out how data will be used to help to achieve those goals and provides actionable plans for where and how to get started.

That last element—action—is critical. Without the ability to act, a data strategy is just another document that will molder away. "It is great to have a strategy, but we have to deliver results, and we have to make a difference for the business," said Floyd Yager of Allstate.

Kolker, formerly of Seattle Children's Hospital, explained that in the healthcare business, especially, the ability to take action is imperative. "One of the lessons we learned the hard way is that data analytics, data science, data modeling is not enough. It's necessary, but we wanted not just to get data and do analytics on it but to get them something which is actionable—actionable insights. We wanted to change the business, and change is very tough, especially in an industry like ours where we're talking about people's lives and health. It's not like somebody's trying to optimize clicks."

In addition to being actionable, a good data strategy must also be flexible: it should be a living document that can adjust as business priorities change and technology evolves and is frequently reviewed and revisited. The kinds of business questions that matter may shift and questions that used to be very difficult to answer may suddenly become low-hanging fruit thanks to a new tool or technique.

When these shifts happen, the data strategy must evolve. That doesn't mean that you chuck it out and start over. Rather, revising the data strategy is about making sure that the tools you're investing in, the capabilities you're building with those tools, and the use cases you're applying those capabilities to all still align with where your business is headed. Subscribing to the notion that data is important isn't enough on its own: what matters is that the business can take concrete steps to put that notion into action.

"The main challenge for organizations that are already there, that are already thinking in that data-driven way," said Amy Gershkoff of Zynga, "is really around how to take the vision of being data-driven and leveraging data science and machine learning, and how to make it a tactical, tractable reality that can be turned from a vision into a shovel-ready roadmap."

There is also the ongoing issue that questions tend to breed other questions. "Invariably, as you answer one question with a particular piece of analysis, it raises five more. And that tends to go on for a while," said Scott Kaylie, formerly of QuestPoint. "At some point, you hit a kind of inflection point where, for certain areas of data or corporate function, you have exhausted a lot of the questions, but there could continually be different forensic type analyses— there is always the potential for some problem to occur in some part of the business. And ideally, you have the flexibility and the capability to use your data to shed light on it, and give you indications of the cause."

The perpetual nature of creating, managing, and implementing a sound data strategy is why the role of the CDO will continue to matter for decades to come.

On data governance

Of course, how the data gets used, particularly in certain settings like hospitals and financial institutions, can be very sensitive. As discussed earlier in this report, the need for regulatory compliance and oversight of what's called data governance— ensuring that data is handled according to strict standards and guidelines—was part of the initial genesis of the CDO role.

While it may seem like a no-brainer to address these issues before anything else, not everything can be done all at once. The ability to organize and prioritize is crucial, and a CDO can bring a lot to the table here.

"On the governance and policy side of things," said Jennifer Ippoliti, formerly of Raymond James, "I have created a central point of escalation for data issues so that we can look at them together. We can prioritize them independently regarding what is best for the enterprise as a whole—and not just one particular user or group of users —and then get that into the technology pipeline so that we can fix things in the order that is best for the firm. That didn't exist before I came along."

She elaborated on her process by naming distinct steps. "There are two sides to the governance: One is making the business decisions and prioritizing them. The other is more of a release-planning exercise, where we work with the different applications groups, determine which ones need to be involved, and then slot the changes into their release cycles in a way that is consistent with all of our policies."

Micheline Casey agreed that working out data governance can be time-consuming. Especially at a place like the Federal Reserve, where powerful banks scrutinize every move all over the world, nothing happens without a lot of careful consideration and conversation; the idea of agile iteration is foreign to an organization full of economists who want to be 100% sure of everything before publication.

Put that way; it's easy to imagine why the CDO would have to have numerous lengthy conversations to put new data policies in place. But the perception is that data governance is almost automatic. "They thought it was like a Chia Pet where you added water and all these data governance policies just sprouted out of thin air," said Casey, "but they realize it's a lot of heavy lifting."

It's so much work, in fact, that some companies who have gotten past that initial perception are employing a Chief Risk Officer to work alongside the CDO and to handle all the data governance responsibilities so that the CDO is free to focus on new products and efficiencies.

Political Challenges

This idea that various perceptions about data can be an obstacle is a very significant one. According to Eugene Kolker, formerly of Seattle Children's Hospital, it's the most significant one. "The main challenge is not technical, it's not on the analytics side, it's not even to get some data from multiple systems (which is extremely complicated in our case)," said Kolker. "It's about people."

During the first year he served as CDO, in fact, Kolker noticed that similar programs his team was running inside the hospital were yielding very different outcomes. "We were thinking, 'they're the same, why is one working and one not?' It was the most crucial angle of people."

After that, his team began to take a more active approach to the human part of the equation. "We're not just focusing on specific tasks, projects, but on specific people who can make decisions and act on them," he said. "We engage people like we are internal consultants, and utilize the best practices in consulting approaches and business processes."

The art of the possible

Charles Thomas of Wells Fargo also sees data evangelism and reaching out to others in the organization as the biggest challenge of the role. "That's been the majority of my time: not convincing them that they should use data, but convincing them that they should use it holistically," he said.

The key to successful persuasion, Thomas added, lies in showing people how they can be even more successful than they currently are. "When you're in a company that has done well, it's showing people the art of the possible. There aren't a lot of things that are broken here. There aren't a lot of things that we're not doing well.

The question is, are we optimizing or doing as well as we possibly could?"

It's also about pulling focus away from the individual agency or division, and back onto the company as a whole: centralization is about more than just data—it's about working for the greater success of the company and pulling in the same direction.

"My job is to help them see the power of their vertical through the lens of the horizontal. In other words, helping them see that playing enterprise ball has a direct benefit to them," said Thomas. "The sub-agencies have all grown up with a certain way of doing data and analytics. It's about, not telling them their approach has been wrong, but their approach is sub-optimized for an enterprise view."

The phrase that Thomas used, "the art of the possible," is one that came up several times in the course of various conversations with CDOs. Prince Otto Eduard Leopold von Bismarck, Duke of Lauenburg, was Prime Minister of Prussia in 1867 when he famously said during an interview, "Politics is the art of the possible." So perhaps what so many CDOs are inadvertently saying is that their job is all about politics—and they wouldn't be wrong. As Otto von Bismarck would go on to oversee the (first) unification of Germany into a single nation, and a good part of the role of CDO is about unifying the various business units into a single data-driven organization, the reference seems particularly apt.

The art of persuasion

Tyrone Grandison, Deputy CDO of the federal Department of Commerce, described his process of bringing people together. "Ideally you have a conversation to lay out options, and you have the entire team decide on what the product is based on the input that you are providing them," said Grandison. "And the input is going to be: I know what the mission is and I know what the business concerns or constraints are; I know what is technically possible; I know the timelines; I know the newer techniques to get this done. Here is what I recommend. Here are the pros and cons. I want your feedback on what your concerns are or what you would do. And having everyone buy-in and own that process, and own the project, and own the outcome."

The mission of the Department of Commerce is simple: to create the conditions for economic growth. But the execution of that mission can be complex. Grandison's team has spun up two hugely successful projects—one internally focused and one externally focused—to further that mission. Internally, the Commerce Data Academy offers a dozen different courses to thousands of department employees to teach and promote data skills. Externally, the Data Usability Project provides open data sets accompanied by both visualizations and tutorials to provide not only data but also contextual knowledge to the public. Such significant undertakings would not be possible without the ability to build consensus and buy-in.

The good news is that, while persuasion may still be necessary regarding the finer points of process or possibility, the overall importance of data is becoming more and more apparent. "Day-to-day it seems to get easier," said Floyd Yager of Allstate. "I like to think some of that is my great influence walking around and talking to people and getting them to see. But I think, quite honestly, a lot of it is that you can't pick up a magazine anymore without there being an article about big data or analytics and how it is changing the world."

REPORTING LINES FOR THE CDO ROLE

The responsibilities outlined above are the central themes that have emerged over a period. The reality is that, for many early CDOs, job responsibility number one was to figure out where they fit and what their other duties should be. The role has sometimes been created without a very specific idea of what the organization hopes to accomplish with data, or how the CDO role should be positioned relative to the existing hierarchy.

Joy Bonaguro experienced this in San Francisco, where the position was mandated by legislation but not well outlined: "Defining and understanding where the role sits in the existing structure was something that had to be done."

Micheline Casey also encountered this at the Federal Reserve Board: "They'd never seen a CDO, and they weren't sure at all what a CDO was supposed to do. They were sure something was needed, but they weren't sure what that looked like, smelled like, tasted like."

So what you find right now is that the reporting structures vary every bit as much as the job responsibilities: some CDOs report directly to the chief executive officer (CEO), while others report to the CTO, CIO, or even the chief financial officer (CFO). Some larger enterprises such as AIG have multiple CDOs, one for each major group, and sometimes also one for the overall conglomerate.

"One of the reasons we see such a variability with CDOs is because you may have one business whose definition is that the CDO is the data steward, and they report to a team within the CIO's office (so they may be one or two levels down from the CIO). On the other end of the spectrum we have a chief data officer who is peer to the chief marketing officer and the chief financial officer, and who is changing the direction of where the organization is going around data and analytics," said Mark Ramsey, former CDO of Samsung.

This latter scenario is the ideal one. Because the ultimate role of the CDO is to use data to support business goals directly, the CDO functions best when it reports directly to the CEO, and is allowed to be a peer at the table with other executives setting direction and strategy. To go back to the earlier analogy of the nervous system: such a system works best when it is wired directly into the brain of the place.

While reporting to the CEO is the best practice, Tyrone Grandison, Deputy CDO of the federal Department of Commerce pointed out, "The question about reporting, although important, should be secondary to how do you empower the CDO to take care of the mission, and how do you make sure they have decision-making capability?"

The CDO and the CIO

Most importantly, the CDO needs to be a peer and close collaborator with the CIO. Although their areas of responsibility certainly converge occasionally, the CDO is responsible for organization-wide policy and data management while the CIO is responsible for information technology and applications, and so it doesn't make sense in the long run for the CDO to be nested under the CIO. Rather, they should be two sides of the same coin.

Conventional wisdom holds that the Chief Information Officer was initially intended to be just that: focused on the flow of information. But over time, the role somehow took a left turn and got bogged down in the technology and infrastructure needed to create and maintain information. Some say the Chief Data Officer is the second shot at that original goal—an executive to manage the creation of insights. "There's a certain irony," said John Akred of Silicon Valley Data Science, "in that the CDO is, in one narrative, around because the CIO has become about financial reports and keeping the lights on, so the CDO is the one about deriving value. Data is a lower-order item than information, and yet the CDO is about information, and the CIO is about data."

None of this is to take away from the important role that the CIO can play. Infrastructure and reports are often critical to the smooth running of the business. But all that technology is the roadway; data science is the engine of the sports car. Without a smooth and solid road to drive on, the car is not going to run very well. But it's the data analysis, not the infrastructure that takes you from point A to point B.

Because of the dependent relationship between data and technology, a CDO and CIO who communicate well and work together closely can help a business become superlative. When they work together seamlessly to turn ideal strategies into practical implementations— to turn used cases into capabilities—that's where the magic happens.

Conversely, when that communication and cooperative relationship is lacking, then disaster can strike. "Let's say you have a CIO with a couple of hundred databases within their portfolio," said Brett Gold- stein, former CDO of the Department of Innovation and Technology for the City of Chicago, where he focused on open data, performance management, and applying data analytics. "You go and give the CDO $20 million, and you say, 'Do something amazing.' There is a danger you will end up with shadow architecture such as a bespoke and nonintegrated warehouse, so it is critical to think about integration and shared services from the beginning."

This view underscores how vital both the roles of the CDO and the CIO are to achieving great value with data, and how critical it is for them to work together well. "I strongly believe in efficiency coupled with smart tooling," said Goldstein. "If there isn't a thoughtful and integrated approach, you run the risk of creating more problems than actual sustainable solutions. However, careful thoughtfulness can lead to strong and sustainable innovation."

This also underscores why the CDO and CIO need to be on equal footing, rather than having one report to the other. As Goldstein said: "You don't want a token CDO who can only talk about big ideas—you want a CDO who can execute upon them. Avoid duplication, avoid shadow architecture, and encourage shared collaboration, but at the same time they need real authority to ensure the ability to produce real results."

It helps to think of data and technology as separate disciplines with an integral relationship. "People believe that data is technology," said Ursula Cottone, CDO of Citizen's Bank. "And the reality is data is more of a process and a lot less technology. The technology just enables you to get to it."

At Citizen's, Cottone and her team face challenges that are familiar to many companies. Until it went public in 2014 in what it touts as "the largest commercial bank initial public offering (IPO) in U.S. history," Citizen's was a subsidiary of RBS, a huge bank with lots of internal business units—and data silos. Now, the task is to improve on the legacy data warehouse to enhance access to data, focus on end-to-end processes, and boost both efficiency and value.

Such a tremendous IPO naturally comes with some seismic cultural shifts in addition to the structural shifts. While the warehousing project is no small task, Cottone is not solely focused on the infrastructure. "The technology is the least important, quite frankly," she said. "What we are doing is about the people and process more than the technology. It is technology that builds the project, but what we are doing is so much more than a project."

Another key aspect of differentiating between data and infrastructure is how they're funded and evaluated. "Understanding the data value chain in a particular organization is one of the most valuable mantras that we have," said John Akred of Silicon Valley Data Science, "because it takes data out of that technology stack queue and talks about creating value in the organization. If data is a cost center, then you want to minimize your Oracle footprint, and that's that— there isn't discussion of getting more value out of your data and driving your top-line revenue."

Even where the CDO is being brought in to perform more of a compliance role, a lot of concerns such as budgeting, ownership, reporting structures, and decision-making authority shift in meaning dramatically when you look at data on a cost basis versus an investment basis that comes with returns. Most CIO organizations still operate as cost centers, but the CDO is all about creating new value: it's about investment.

To keep the CDO free to focus on creating that value— going after the carrot of new products and efficiencies—some organizations are bringing on a new executive position focused on data governance and compliance.

Enter the Chief Risk Officer

Some organizations are beginning to add a third role to the mix, to work in partnership with a CDO and CIO: the Chief Risk Officer, or CRO. Sometimes called the Chief Risk Management Officer (CRMO), this role predates the Chief Data Officer by about a decade: the first one seems to have been appointed in 1993, compared with roughly 2002 for the first CDO. What's new is the emergence of a kind of trifecta: CIO, CDO, and CRO all working together.

The role of the CRO saw a surge in the wake of the financial crisis of 2007–2008. Many financial services companies realized that there was a missing piece in how information was being relayed to their boards. The issue wasn't just data and the quality of that data, but how that was constructed into a message and conveyed to the people who needed to know, for example, that their portfolios were unhedged and completely in the equity markets.

"In a highly regulated world, there's been a rise in the role of a Chief Risk Officer," said Senior and Retired President and CEO of Blue Cross Life Insurance Company of Canada James Gilligan. "And I see a place where the CRO will work more collaboratively with the CDO."

This change may be welcome for those concerned with the aftermath of a data breach. Chetan Conikee is CDO of Cloud Physics, an IT solutions provider. He's noticed that even though many companies task their CDOs with overseeing data governance, very rarely is it a CDO in front of the press after something has gone wrong with sensitive data.

"CDO is a relatively new role, and there is no proper definition of the role regarding accountability," he said. "Given that a CDO's role is partitioned between reporting lines, it becomes hard to measure the efficacy of their function. This can be remediated by assigning one core function to the CDO, then watching them streamline operations around this core function and observing how they work in concert with the CIO/CEO to resolve and communicate incidents."

Some would argue that the core function assigned to the CDO should be data strategy—and that data governance and the management of risk and data security should be left in the hands of the CRO.

It's not just the risks inherent with data that connect the CRO to the CDO; it's also the concept of taking data-derived insights and messaging them for the right audience: of translating between technology and the business. There is a natural overlap there that makes the CRO a great ally for the CDO. And of course, the CRO is also a great ally for the CIO when it comes to issues of data security and securing the necessary locks not just on the perimeter of the infrastructure but also the interior of certain applications to ensure that access is restricted to appropriate parties only.

Therefore, as the role of the CDO settles more and more into the emerging best practices, keep an eye not only on the CIO but also on the CRO. "The role of the CRO is continuing to evolve also," said Gilligan, "and the bounds are not clear there. Both the CDO and the CRO are moving in parallel to a more stable future."

Data Stewards

The CDO must be able to work closely with people outside of the executive team, as well. While not an official part of the CDO's reporting structure, and perhaps not even a dotted line, data stewards also have a crucial relationship with the CDO.

The concept of data stewardship derives from a much more traditional model of data management; organizations that already have data stewards in place tend to be fairly large and established. The idea is to put multiple domain experts in charge of their respective kinds of data—the sales manager would be the data steward of customer relationship management (CRM) data, for example.

"We look at the senior level managers—and in some cases mid-level managers of critical lines of business—as our data stewards," said Michael Kelly of the University of South Carolina. "Ultimately in our model of data governance, data stewards have final authority and make decisions about what does or does not happen with the data they are responsible for."

Data stewards work closest to where the data is collected, and are often the ones who best understand the various dimensions of the data, and which standards it should meet. On the one hand, stewards may be able to provide important information to the CDO about how to make sure the best, cleanest data is what gets centralized and shared across the rest of the organization—because they have domain expertise that makes the quality of that data intuitively obvious.

On the other hand, data quality is relative: you always have to ask, "For what purpose?" For example: if your goal is condition monitoring, and you understand that temperature sensors degrade in quality, then you might "correct" that data on the way in because quality in that scenario means accuracy. But if a manufacturer later wants to analyze which supplier has provided the best sensor, that can't be done with data that was "corrected." In other words, the definition of data quality may be different for one use case than for another, depending on what question is being answered.

"The CDO is in a really good place to manage these issues," said John Akred of Silicon Valley Data Science. "The person in the silo is not going to think about the trade-offs of how their data will be used in another place."

Just as the CDO creates significant value by partnering with the CIO on technology investments, and also by partnering with the CRO on regulatory compliance, they can also create significant value by partnering with data stewards on data quality. Data stewards are also key stakeholders embedded in the various business units, and working closely with them is a good way to make sure that projects stay closely aligned not only with the whole enterprise but also with individual departments.

"Whatever it is that you are trying to do with data," said Kelly, "make sure it is going to be of service to the core business, and that your core business is involved in making those decisions. That is what data stewardship gets for us.

LESSONS LEARNED FROM EARLY ADOPTERS

O rganizations that invest wisely in establishing the office of the Chief Data Officer are well positioned to create value for their customers and shareholders. We offer recommendations for executives that outline the strategic and tactical actions needed to drive long-term value for the Chief Data Officer role.

When the CDO is free from concerns about maintenance of current systems or the challenges of rapidly advancing technology, he or she can instead be laser-focused on finding the best ways to put data to work to drive compelling value.

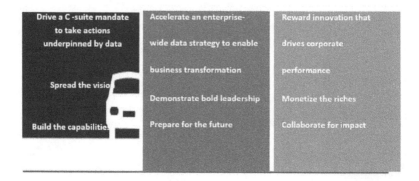

Figure: Three key steps help executives accelerate growth and innovation through the use of data by implementing the role of the Chief Data Officer.

To be clear, a CDO is not a C-level role designed to manage data projects. Instead, the CDO should be a change agent identifying opportunities to leverage and enrich existing data, tap into new data sources and monetize data. Appointing executives to ensure the CDO encompasses a powerful combination of business acumen, technical understanding, and strong negotiation skills.

It's also important to allocate enough resources for the CDO to be effective, including both staff and budget. A CDO without resources — tasked to rally the organization but unable to effect change — is set up to fail.

Drive a C-suite mandate to take actions underpinned by data

The organization takes its direction from the top. If there is a commitment to decision making and operations based on data, that commitment must be clear in all communications emanating from the C-suite, from written messages to executive-led meetings to performance goals.

The Chief Data Officer must be fully empowered to drive value from data, and such empowerment requires both responsibility and authority. At the same time, the appointing organization needs to focus on identifying talent and developing the types of capabilities needed by a data-driven organization.

Spread the vision

The C-suite must share the vision of data-based leadership and drive adoption across the enterprise. We suggest the CDO organization be launched with a broad-based communications and organizational change management plan to support and help ensure common understanding, alignment and enforcement of enterprise values.

Leadership: Demonstrate technology and business integration through leadership experienced in driving the value of data organization-wide.

Integration: Include data/business integration in C-suite executive measurement, and cascade down through the organization via formal performance metrics to help ensure alignment with organizational strategy.

Factual basis: Re-engineer and reorganize around fact-based decision-making processes supporting enterprise performance tied to established data sources, definitions (terms and calculations) and financial measures.

Build the capabilities

A data-driven organization needs leadership with the right combination of business and technical expertise; it requires a focused data team with similarly blended skills, and it requires a corporate culture that recognizes and nurtures those skills.

Share platform: Embed analytics across the enterprise using a common framework, certified data and analytic approaches, provided by a shared platform to drive a performance culture that acts on data-driven insights.

Focus on T-shaped talent: Focus on identifying cross-functional talent with business acumen and data or analytics skills (the two sides of the "T") who can work alongside business units and across organizational boundaries.

Establish career paths: Establish career paths that facilitate movement between business and technical roles to create future data professionals and leaders with keen business insights.

Accelerating An Enterprise-Wide Data Strategy

There is no harder job for a corporate leader than transformation. Although leading a data-driven transformation initiative may seem daunting, a CDO can accelerate the process with purpose and persistence by building a personal network of advisors to bring an outside perspective and by celebrating small wins that reaffirm progress. The CDO should take the lead to develop an organization supporting the strategic use of data, including information governance, enterprise decision-making authority and operational support structures (policy, funding, people, process, technology) for owning, operating and governing strategic data and projects.

Demonstrate bold leadership

CDOs must display motivational and passionate leadership to inspire others and multiple impacts. Powered by a compelling vision, they should be architects, mentors, and connectors who can drive lasting value in the organization.

Create alignment: Create and enforce alignment to an enterprise transformation roadmap and value-based business cases for prioritized data initiatives. Establish an environment where all executives must help chart the new course with strong commitment.

Communicate wins: Identify opportunities for early, small victories, and pursue them aggressively to win enterprise support while the transformation is in process. Communicate major steps in the process.

Create momentum: Engage employees to tap into the available data, guide them in ways to derive valuable insights and take fast action. Launch employee programs that provide training on the skills needed to capitalize on the organization's data assets, and create communities to share ideas and techniques on how to integrate insights into business processes.

Prepare for the future

Protecting an organization's critical information is vital to its stock price and market share. With rising numbers of data breaches, organizations without a clear strategy will put their data, brand, reputation and, potentially, their customer relationships at risk. The CDO should charter and lead a business-driven data governance council around clear, tangible goals and measurable business outcomes and objectives.

Share responsibilities: Convey an organization-wide sense of ownership to manage data quality, create a data quality culture and drive value with simplification, data sharing, management and reuse.

Define standards: Define and govern data security, compliance, and privacy standards organization-wide. The Chief Information Security Officer (or comparable role, if there is no CISO) should be prepared to work with the CDO to define and manage data security and privacy policies and practices.

Protect critical data: Protect and safeguard data from cybersecurity threats, data breaches, and exposure of private information. Data protection itself should be adequately funded to guard against breaches, increase compliance and protect the reputation of the organization.

Reward Innovation That Drives Corporate Performance

Many corporations struggle to determine how to use limited resources and existing data to generate the greatest possible impact. Effective CDOs must develop the art of scanning the data environment to identify and capitalize on what they find quickly. When future benefits and payback windows are a longer term from data-related innovation, a CDO must connect the dots and link back to the strategic intent and goals of the organization to drive sponsorship.

Monetize the riches

The CDO should take the reins as the chief innovator for driving value from data. He or she must develop a clear view of data and data-related projects across the organization and drive new efficiencies through shared information, common tools and an understanding of data. Also, the CDO should be aggressive in seeking out new sources of information — within or beyond the organization — that could open new markets or new opportunities for growth.

Create quick wins: Generate momentum and commitment with visible and rapid results from data investments. Challenge conventional wisdom and focus on opportunities for innovation by showcasing wins at an enterprise level.

Disseminate learning: Determine what is working and what isn't, and disseminate the knowledge and methods of achieving the best results.

Measure outcomes: Prioritize resource allocation by measuring business outcomes, and create a feedback loop for optimizing future investments by tracking business cases through and after delivery to help ensure promises are kept. Develop internal systems and process metrics that can capture relevant results.

Collaborate for impact

Successful collaborations include a diverse array of stakeholders but also involve complex human and organizational issues. To avoid delays, a CDO must establish a shared vision and governance model and nurture a culture of trust without which even the best-intentioned efforts can be undermined.

Clear pathways: Convert shared vision and individual passion into an action plan. Embrace new ways of working to share data by clearly defining common objectives and transcending parochialism.

Build trust: Bring diverse line of business functions together to drive a challenging, stimulating and catalytic atmosphere for innovation and monetization. Quantify how the shared efforts drive down costs or generate revenues for each function, and prioritize projects accordingly.

Explore new partnerships: Explore avenues and partnerships that abound outside the organization to incorporate new and diverse sources to enrich existing data. Optimize the effort by focusing on both processes and outcomes.

The Availability Gap

While many universities are now adding business classes to their data programs—and vice versa—today's graduates won't be ready for executive hiring until long after tomorrow. According to management consultants Russell Reynolds Associates, "The spike in demand for Chief Digital Officers has been felt globally. In Europe, the number of search requests for this role has risen by almost a third in the last 24 months. The United States has seen the same growth in half that time." So we're facing an inevitable gap during which companies must be even more diligent about preparing properly for the hiring process: mapping out their priorities and goals and understanding which skills need to run deep and which can be learned on the job or acquired through collaboration.

There are also some things you can do to make your company and the role of CDO within it as appealing as possible to qualified candidates. The first and most important is to know why you want one, as explained above: to understand what your goal is in hiring a CDO, and to be committed to that goal.

"The exciting thing for CDOs, and what's going to attract the ideal CDO, is a situation where there is a real opportunity to transform the business," said Mark Ramsey, formerly of Samsung. "Where the company is really serious, they are committed, and they are looking for ways to really transform, those will be the ones that will attract the top-performing CDOs—as opposed to sort of, 'Hey, everybody is getting a CDO, and we probably need to have one, too, and we'll get some incremental benefit out of it."

In the most ideal and dramatic cases, the CDO is there to help usher in a shift from data as a cost center to data as an asset—from an operational use of data to a strategic use of it.

As discussed, the most successful CDOs are the ones who have the business acumen to understand what needs to happen in order to support business objectives; the technical skills to select the right tools and techniques to make it happen; and the diplomacy to get the buy-in needed to get everyone else pulling in the same direction. They are there to help usher in a major shift, from an operational use of data to a strategic use of data. When that happens, the only possible outcome is a tremendous change. To successfully make this shift requires the organization to change the mindset, a change in infrastructure, and a change in the alignment of incentives.

The CDO is there to help drive these changes, but ultimately they have to come from the very top: from the CEO down. "The one ingredient that has been critical in every single initiative: you need a CEO who is all-in, who is vested with unwavering commitment and support," said Barbara Cohn, former CDO of New York State. "It makes all the difference."

A company that's open to change embraces the kind of experimentation that allows for true innovation to happen. That sounds exciting at first glance, but you have to remember that the nature of experiments is that they often fail. Embracing experimentation means being willing also to embrace failure, and that notion can be a lot less appealing. But good experimentation design makes sure that there is something to learn from each failure. So it is often a matter of changing company culture to allow for, and even celebrate, the kinds of experiments that breed helpful failures and iteration toward outstanding successes.

"In the press, there is so much hype about machine learning and data science that a person who hasn't worked closely with data science before may come in with an unrealistic set of expectations about the value it can drive without proper investment in technology, infrastructure, and talent," said Amy Gershkoff of Zynga. "It is important for executives to understand that driving value from data science is a journey, and it takes time and investment—but if you are on the right journey, investing in the necessary infrastructure, and you are testing and learning as you go, you can drive tremendous value for the business over the long-term."

If you are truly open to this kind of change and experimentation inside your organization, and you can demonstrate that to the right CDO candidate, then your company could wind up on par with the Amazons and Googles of the world, using data to disrupt entire industries—and shape the future.

Moving forward with the role of CDO

We are indeed just at the beginning of a big data boom that is undeniable, irreversible and loaded with opportunity for organizations that transform themselves with data-driven decisions. And the Chief Data Officer position is a crucial element in helping organizations realize and manage the full value of their information assets.

As what today is known as "big data" becomes the norm, organizations of all sizes will adjust to the new reality in which timely access to high-quality data, a keen understanding of data and smart actions based on insights define winners and losers in the marketplace. The number of CDOs is likely to grow rapidly — across more organizations in more industries around the world. Already, organizations are changing responsibilities within the C-suite, creating a new CDO role to manage their data. With data recognized as an enterprise asset, the creation of a data policy and an information governance team would not be considered complete without the appointment of a leader who manages this asset, regardless of the name given the role.

As CDOs become more comfortable in their roles, overcome issues and celebrate successes, they will have more and more opportunities to network, exchange stories and establish best practices on a broad basis. Some of the best CDOs will emerge as role models. And as young professionals aspire to the role, they will steer their careers to build the combination of business and technical experience that helps create a strong CDO.

But the real measure of CDO success will be whether they help drive value from data. Most important, the CDO cannot afford to be risk averse and should be ready to assess opportunities and, as appropriate, venture into new areas, through fact-driven and imagination-inspired approaches. If in the not-too-distant future, case studies of CDO success abound, those organizations that got an early start in establishing the office and building an effective organization will stand to reap the benefits. For that reason, now is the time to begin an evaluation of the CDO role and its potential impact.

The best CDO's act as connectors and not the dots

REFERENCES

➤ http://data.consilium.europa.eu/doc/document/ST-5419-2016-INIT/en/pdf

➤ http://image-src.bcg.com/BCG_COM/BCG-Staying-the-Course-in-Banking-Mar-2017_tcm9-146794.pdf

➤ National Information Center. A repository of financial data and information on banks and other financial institutions collected by the Federal Reserve as of 12/31/16

➤ http://www.gartner.com/smarterwithgartner/keys-to-success-for-chief-data-officers/

➤ http://www.payscale.com/college-salary-report/common-jobs-for-majors/engineering

➤ http://www.pwc.com/us/en/financial-services/publications/viewpoints/assets/pwc-chief-data-officer-cdo.pdf

➤ https://www.wired.com/insights/2014/07/rise-chief-data-officer/

➢ https://www.forbes.com/sites/kimberlywhitler/2016/10/22/what-is-a-chief-data-officer-and-why-do-firms-need-them/#2be1e81cbc94

➢ http://www.cio.co.uk/it-leadership/cio-cdo-differences-3644709/

➢ http://www.informationweek.com/strategic-cio/it-strategy/rise-and-fall-of-the-chief-data-officer/a/d-id/1324280

➢ http://insights.dice.com/2016/03/15/how-much-do-tech-bosses-really-earn/2/

➢ http://whatis.techtarget.com/reference/Roles-and-responsibilities-guide-What-does-a-CIO-do

➢ https://techcrunch.com/2015/07/07/dont-hire-a-chief-data-officer-unless-youre-serious-about-becoming-a-data-driven-company/